Mohammedanism

Mohammedanism

An Historical Survey

H. A. R. GIBB

Second Edition

OXFORD UNIVERSITY PRESS
London Oxford New York

First published in the Home University Library, 1949
Second edition published 1953
First issued as an Oxford University Press paperback, 1962
Reprinted with revisions, 1970
This reprint, 1973
Printed in the United States of America

Preface

THE ORIGINAL volume of Mohammedanism in this series was written by Professor D. S. Margoliouth, and published in 1911. After the lapse of thirty-five years, a restatement of the subject is called for rather than a re-edition of the original work.

Between one generation and the next, the bases of judgement necessarily suffer some change. They are modified firstly in the material or scientific sense, by the discovery of new facts and the increase of understanding which results from the broadening and deepening of research. If this were all, it might well be met by minor additions or alterations in the text. More important, however, is the change in the spiritual and imaginative sense. Every work of this kind reflects not only the factual knowledge but also the intellectual and emotional limitations of its period, even when every effort is made to eliminate prejudgement and prejudice. No generation in our changing world sees the problems of life, society, or belief in terms of the thought or values of the previous generation; and the gulf which separates the outlook of 1911 from the outlook of 1946 is one which has rarely been equalled in so short a space of human history.

Inevitably, then, such a book as this aims to be will be permeated by the intellectual modes and the unconscious prejudices of its age. But even these limitations may to some extent distinguish it (not necessarily to its advantage) from the generality of books published on its subject. Most writers approach the subject of Mohammedanism from one or other of two opposed points of view, neither of which is free from conscious prejudgement nor fully adjusted to the prevailing intellectual climate. The one group approaches from the angle of apologetic, the other *de haut en bas*. The former writers are mainly professing Muslims, who are concerned to defend their faith and its associated culture from the variety of indictments which have been laid against it, and to counter-attack their opponents. The loyalty and sincerity which inspire these works deserve respect, and as religious documents they have their due importance. But it is difficult to find amongst them one which appreciates the issues and meets them on the level of current thought.

The second group of writings emanate from those whose view is coloured by the belief that Islam is an inferior religion. Where this view arises from a sincere religious faith, it too may often deserve respect. This is the case with most missionary literature, and it would be unjust not to recognize the great advances which have been made amongst missionaries in recent years towards substituting a sympathetic entering-into the religious experience of the Muslim for the crude externality of their former approach. Yet the element of pre-judgement is inherent in their attitude towards Islam, and it cannot be left out of account in any assessment of their writings.

It would be vain to hope that either of these groups will look with favour upon an exposition which will serve the interests of neither. It need only be added that the present work has been consciously influenced by two convictions; one that Islam is an autonomous expression of religious thought and experience, which must be viewed in and through itself and its own principles and standards; the other, that while the practice of every religion to some extent falls short of its own highest ideals, the exposition of an outside observer should lay more stress upon the ideals which it strives to realize than upon the failings of our common humanity.

In order to distinguish this volume in the Home University Library from its predecessor, the phrase 'An Historical Survey' has been added to the title. Only through its history is it possible to gain an understanding of any long-established system of belief, or to appreciate the issues with which Islam is confronted today and the forces with which it is equipped to meet them.

OXFORD.
January 1948

Note to the Second Edition

A NUMBER of passages, especially in Chapters 5 and 6, have been re-written in this edition in the light of recent studies. The emergence of Pakistan as a new Muslim State has also necessitated some changes in detail, and the Bibliography has been revised.

The writer would like to take this opportunity to express his thanks for the encouraging messages received from many friends, both Muslim and non-Muslim.

OXFORD.
October 1952.

The publication of this book in paperback has given the writer an opportunity to make a number of small changes in the text, and to take account of recent publications in the Bibliography.

OXFORD.
April 1968

Contents

1 The Expansion of Islam   1

2 Mohammed   16

3 The Koran   24

4 Doctrine and Ritual in the Koran   36

5 The Tradition of the Prophet   49

6 The Sharīʿa   60

7 Orthodoxy and Schism   73

8 Sūfism   86

9 The Sūfi Orders   100

10 Islam in the Modern World   113

Bibliography   132

Index   139

1

The Expansion of Islam

THE OLD legend that Islam was born of the desert is taking a long time to die. Since Renan popularized the view that monotheism is the 'natural religion of the desert', it seemed a plausible argument that Mohammed's insistence on the unity and unapproachable greatness of God was simply a reflection of the vast changeless wastes of Arabia. More recent research has shown up the falsity of this imaginative dogma. Neither in its origins nor in its early development had the desert any creative part in it. The Arabian colouring which has clung to Islam came not so much through the direct social influence of its early Arabian environment and Arab adherents as from the Arabic Koran and the intellectual bias which this gave to the nascent Muslim culture.

The word *Islām*, finally adopted by Mohammed as the distinctive name of the faith which he preached, means 'submitting [oneself or one's person to God]'. The adherent of Islam is usually designated by the corresponding adjective *Muslim* (of which *Moslem* is a Western adaptation). The Persians adopted a different adjective *Musalmān,* from which are derived the Anglo-Indian *Mussulman* and French *Musulman*. Modern Muslims dislike the terms Mohammedan and Mohammedanism, which seem to them to carry the implication of worship of Mohammed, as Christian and Christianity imply the worship of Christ.

Probably no well-informed person now shares the belief of our medieval forefathers that the 'Turks and infidels' worshipped 'Mahomet' in the form of an idol—a double error, since any image

or visual symbol in religious worship is anathema to Muslims. Yet
the term Mohammedan is not in itself unjustified, and in a less
self-conscious age Muslims were proud to call their community
al-umma al-Muhammadīya. Of the two articles of the basic pro-
fesssion of the Muslim faith, 'There is but one God and Mohammed
is His Apostle', the first may be assented to by many besides
Muslims, whereas it is the second which distinguishes Islam from all
other faiths. For its implication is not that Mohammed was *an*
Apostle, one amongst many, but that in Mohammed the series of
Apostles reached its culmination and that the Koran revealed
through him is the final and unchangeable revelation of the Divine
Will, abrogating all previous records of revelation. No one since his
time who does not hold this belief and all that follows from it is
entitled to call himself a Muslim or to share the privileges of
membership of the Brotherhood of Islam. Conversely, the orthodox
exponents of Islam have generally maintained that no one who
publicly professes these articles can be declared a non-Muslim.

Although the beginnings of Islam go back to Mohammed's
preaching in his native city of Mecca, the latent characteristics of
the faith were developed only after his move to Medina in the year
A.D. 622. Before his death ten years later it had become clear that
Islam was not simply a body of private religious beliefs, but involved
the setting-up of an independent community, with its own system
of government, laws, and institutions. That the 'Emigration' (*Hijra*)
marked a turning-point in history was recognized already by the
first generation of Muslims, who adopted the year 622 as the first
year of the new Mohammedan era.

With a strong and skilful government and a faith to inspire its
followers and its armies, it was not long before the new community
controlled all Western Arabia and looked round for new worlds to
conquer. After a slight backwash on the death of Mohammed, the
wave of conquest swept over Northern and Eastern Arabia and
broke audaciously upon the outposts of the Eastern Roman Empire
in Transjordan and of the Persian Empire in Southern Iraq. The
forces of the two gigantic Empires, exhausted by long warfare
against one another, were defeated one after the other in a series of
rapid and brilliant campaigns. Within six years of Mohammed's

death all Syria and Iraq were tributary to Medina, and in four years
more Egypt was added to the new Muslim Empire.

These astonishing victories, the precursors of still wider conquests
which were to carry the Arabs in less than a century into Morocco,
Spain, and France, to the gates of Constantinople, far across Central Asia and up to the Indus river, confirmed the character of
Islam as a strong, self-confident, conquering faith. From this came
its unyielding, and even hostile, attitude to everything that lay
outside itself, but also its record of broad tolerance of diversity
within its own community, refusal to persecute those of other communities, and the dignity with which it has endured moments of
eclipse.

But still more astonishing than the speed of the conquests was
their orderly character. Some destruction there must have been
during the years of warfare, but by and large the Arabs, so far from
leaving a trail of ruin, led the way to a new integration of peoples
and cultures. The structure of law and government which
Mohammed had bequeathed to his successors, the Caliphs, proved its
value in controlling these Bedouin armies. Islam emerged into the
civilized outer world, not as the crude superstition of marauding
hordes, but as a moral force that commanded respect and a coherent
doctrine that could challenge on their own ground the Christianity
of East Rome and the Zoroastrianism of Persia. It is true that the
tribal instincts and traditions of the Bedouin broke out from time
to time in revolts and civil wars; but in the end they served only to
affirm more effectively the strength and the will to order of the new
imperial power.

To the peoples of the conquered countries the Arab supremacy
signified at first little more than a change of masters. There was
no breach in the continuity of their life and social institutions, no
persecution, no forced conversion. But little by little Islam began to
modify the old social structure of Western Asia and Egypt, and Arab
elements to penetrate the old Hellenistic and Persian cultures. The
Arab colonies planted in the newly-won territories were not merely
garrison towns and headquarters of armies; they were also centres
from which the new religion was propagated. Enriched by the
wealth drawn from the subject provinces and swelled by the constant

influx of converts, they became the matrices of the new Islamic civilization.

Already in 660 the capital of the Arab Empire had shifted to Damascus, the seat of the new dynasty of Caliphs of the Umayyad House. While Medina remained the centre of Muslim religious learning, the government and public life of the Empire was influenced by the Hellenistic tradition of East Rome. This first stage of interaction with the older civilizations is symbolized by the two exquisite monuments of the Umayyad age, the Great Mosque of Damascus and the Dome of the Rock at Jerusalem, as well as by the sudden profusion of sects and heresies in the 'new provinces'. But the ultimate consequence was a cleavage between the religious and secular institutions of the Muslim community, which sapped the foundations of the Umayyad Caliphate and, reinforced by the grievances of the non-Arab subjects and the outbreak of a civil war between the Arab tribes, brought about its downfall in A.D. 750.

Such a conflict, however, demonstrates that in the century that had elapsed since the death of Mohammed the religious culture of Islam had itself undergone a considerable development and consolidation both inside and outside Arabia. A great religious teacher on the one hand represents the culmination of a spiritual process. He sums up its essentials and so vitalizes them by his personality and his insight that they come to his fellow-men as a revelation of new truth. On the other hand, he stands at the beginning of a new spiritual process, whose width and depth are determined not so much by his own vision as by the spiritual insight of his followers and their capacity to develop his teaching. Still more is this the case when the original teaching expands over wide areas outside its original home, and in contact with other deep-rooted cultures and civilizations is subjected to those interactions and pressures to which all living organisms are exposed.

The new tensions which were created in and by Islam and the new spiritual standards and ideals which it set up will be analysed in their proper place. Here we are concerned only to note the immediate release of intellectual energies which paralleled the expansion of the Arabs into the outer world. The vitality of the imprint made by Mohammed on the minds of his followers is shown by the cultural stimulus which it gave—in the first instance, of course, within the field of the religious movement itself. In assimilating and expanding the new teaching, system and method were introduced into the intellectual life of the Arabs. New sciences were founded: the study of the Prophetic Tradition, philology, history, and above all law. The transformation is amazing when one looks back at the intellectual poverty and isolation of Medina a bare hundred years before, still more when it is remembered that this was in the main the work of Arabs themselves, building upon the foundations laid by Mohammed, self-evolved with none but the most meagre external influences.

This was the fundamental and decisive contribution of the Arabs to the new Muslim culture. To its material civilization they contributed little. That began its brilliant career when the dynasty of Abbasid Caliphs succeeded to the Umayyads and founded their new capital of Baghdad in 762. The first age of external conquest was over, and to it succeeded an age of internal expansion. The ninth and tenth centuries witnessed the climax of Islamic civilization in breadth and creative effort. Industry, commerce, architecture, and the minor arts flourished with immense vitality as Persia, Mesopotamia, Syria, and Egypt brought their contribution to the common stock.

These new energies found an outlet in intellectual life as well. While the religious sciences continued to develop in a score of new centres strung out from Samarqand to North Africa and Spain, literature and thought, drawing upon Greek, Persian, and even Indian sources, broke out in new directions, often independent of the Muslim tradition and more or less in revolt against the narrowness of the orthodox system. Under the stimulus of the widening physical and intellectual horizons the material and the spiritual were interacting at the highest pressure.

It is difficult to indicate in a few words the many-sided intellectual activities of this age. The older 'Muslim sciences' of history and philology broadened out to embrace secular history and belles-lettres. Greek medical and mathematical science were made accessible in a library of translations and were developed by Persian and Arab scholars, especially in algebra, trigonometry, and optics.

Geography—perhaps the most sensitive barometer of culture—flowered in all its branches, political, organic, mathematical, astronomical, natural science, and travel, and reached out to embrace the lands of civilizations of far-distant peoples.

While these new sciences touched only the fringes of the religious culture, the inroads of Greek logic and philosophy inevitably produced a sharp and bitter conflict, which came to a head in the third Islamic century. The leaders of Islam saw its spiritual foundations endangered by the subtle infidelities of pure rationalism, and although they ultimately triumphed over the Hellenizing school, philosophy always remained an object of suspicion in their eyes, even when it came to be studied merely as an apologetic tool. More serious still, however, were the further consequences of their victory —the growth in theological circles of a kind of jealousy of any intellectual pursuit which was purely secular or ventured beyond the range of their control.

Such a deliberate narrowing-down of intellectual interests had one peculiar effect. The religious sciences rested on a foundation of Arabic philology, and Arabic philology was based upon the old pre-Islamic poetry. Just as the learning of Western Christianity in the Middle Ages was based exclusively upon Latin, and thus preserved in uneasy partnership with the Christian tradition the poetry, mythology, and social heritage of Rome, so the Muslim scholar steeped himself in the literary and social heritage of the ancient Arabs. Their virtues were idealized, their proverbs supplied the staple of popular ethics. That the whole of Muslim literature in its first four formative centuries was written in Arabic, and that it was pervaded at all points by this Arab tradition, are the factors chiefly responsible for the enduring Arabian impress upon Islamic culture.

The struggle to subordinate all intellectual life to the authority of religion went on for many centuries in successive regions of the Muslim world. Where no fresh stiumulus arose to prolong and revive flagging energies, the religious culture caught all other intellectual activities on the rebound, and by minor concessions held them and converted them into its own instruments. Those which it could not use, such as medicine and mathematics, stagnated or ultimately died away. But from time to time fresh outbursts of creative activity, like that in Muslim Spain in the eleventh and twelfth centuries, bore witness to the continuing absorptive and expansive power of the Islamic civilization.

Yet again, the assertion of the supremacy of the religious culture could not have succeeded had the culture not offered within itself enough scope for the active exercise of the intellectual faculties. The study which in some sense took the place of the discarded sciences was not, however, theology. The master science of the Muslim world was Law. Law, indeed, might be said to embrace all things, human and divine, and both for its comprehensiveness and for the ardour with which its study was pursued it would be hard to find a parallel elsewhere, except in Judaism.

But apart altogether from its intellectual pre-eminence and scholastic function, Islamic Law was the most far-reaching and effective agent in moulding the social order and the community life of the Muslim peoples. By its very comprehensiveness it exerted a steady pressure upon all private and social activities, setting a standard to which they conformed more and more closely as time went on, in spite of the resistance of ancient habits and time-honoured customs, especially amongst the more independent nomadic and mountain tribes. Moreover, Islamic Law gave practical expression to the characteristic Muslim quest for unity. In all essentials it was uniform, although the various schools differed in points of detail. To its operation was due the striking convergence of social ideals and ways of life throughout the medieval Muslim world. It went far deeper than Roman law; by reason of its religious bases and its theocratic sanctions it was the spiritual regulator, the conscience, of the Muslim community in all its parts and activities.

This function of law acquired still greater significance as political life in the Muslim world swung ever further away from the theocratic ideal of Mohammed and his successors. The decline of the Abbasid Caliphate in the tenth and eleventh centuries opened the door to political disintegration, the usurpation of royal authority by local princes and military governors, the rise and fall of ephemeral dynasties, and repeated outbreaks of civil war. But however seriously the political and military strength of the vast Empire might be weakened, the moral authority of the Law was but the more enhanced and held the social fabric of Islam compact and secure through all the fluctuations of political fortune.

At the end of the tenth century, the geographical area of Islam was but little wider than it had been in 750. But a great civilization had been built up, brilliant in intellectual life, wealthy and enterprising in economic life, powerfully cemented by an authoritative Law—the whole a visible embodiment of the temporal and spiritual might of Islam. As its military strength declined, it, like the Roman Empire six centuries before, fell gradually under the domination of the barbarians from beyond its frontiers, but also, like the Roman Empire, imposed upon the barbarians its religion, its law, and respect for its civilization.

These barbarians were Turkish tribesmen from Central Asia. The same westward pressure that had carried the Bulgars, Magyars, Comans, and Patzinaks into Southern Russia and Eastern Europe carried other tribes into Persia and westward into Iraq and Anatolia. The work of conversion to Islam had begun while they were still in their Central Asian homelands; consequently, the establishment of Turkish Sultanates in Western Asia made at first little outward difference to the domestic life of the Muslim community. The first result was a fresh military expansion; south-eastwards into Northern India, north-westwards into Asia Minor. Simultaneously, in the far West, nomadic Berber tribesmen were carrying Islam into the fringes of Negro Africa in the Senegal and Niger basins, while nomadic Arab tribesmen, no longer controlled by the religious authority of the early Caliphs, were destroying by pillage and neglect the centres of civilization that their Arab predecessors had built on the debris of Roman and Byzantine Africa.

The resurgence of the nomadic elements in all parts of the Muslim world confronted the Muslim community with a problem which has close analogies with the problem of the Christian Church confronted by the Germanic kingdoms. Islam had grown up within the framework of an urban civilization. Its social background was the settled life of the centralized State, and so strong had this tradition become that, as the example just mentioned shows, its influence amongst even the Bedouin Arabs had dwindled away. It was now faced with the task of making the religious order and culture effective within a social structure in which tribalism predominated. The old solution (dating back to Mohammed himself), to force or beguile the tribesmen into settled life, could now be applied at most only to the small group of ruling tribes who formed the retinue and officers of the Sultan in the new capital cities. Although the Sultans themselves were often enthusiastic Muslims, and their governments within two or three generations conformed to the normal patterns of the settled communities into which they had come, they were seldom able to maintain complete control over their nomadic or semi-nomadic followers.

This task of preventing the social and cultural disintegration of Islam and of bringing the tribesmen within the radius of its civilizing and cohesive forces was met by a new instrument which had been forged among the urban populations during the preceding centuries. By this time the pressure of Muslim doctrine and practice had mastered most of the resistances that had, at an earlier time, sought an outlet in heterodox and subversive movements. But this did not lead to stagnation. On the contrary, the devotional feeling of the townsmen, grinding a channel of its own, burst the bonds of the orthodox disciplines and found a new freedom in the ranges of mysticism. From the eleventh century onwards mysticism enlisted in its service a large proportion of the vital spiritual energies of the Muslim community, and created within Islam a fount of self-renewal which maintained its spiritual vigour through all the later centuries of political and economic decay.

The growth and development of Sūfism (to give this movement its proper name) display many of the characteristic features of Islamic culture. It welled up from below, by the spontaneous action of individual citizens, mostly of the urban artisan classes. No formal authorization or recognition was asked for or received—at first, indeed, there was much opposition from the learned and some persecution. It remained autonomous and personal and only after some centuries of growth began to organize itself in institutional forms. Above all, in the tension between the element of rigidity represented by the Sacred Law and the element of flexibility arising out of the spiritual intuition of the individual, it conformed to the pattern

which runs through all the spiritual and cultural manifestations of
Islam.

The mystics, whether as individual missionaries or (later on) as
members of organized brotherhoods, were the leaders in the task
of conversion among the pagans and the superficially Islamized
tribes. The most successful missions were often those of co-nationals
of the tribesmen, uncouth, illiterate, and crude though many of them
were. They laid the foundations upon which in later generations
the refining influences of orthodox law and theology could be
brought to bear. It was mainly due to them that through successive
centuries the religious frontiers of Islam were steadily extended in
Africa, in India and Indonesia, across Central Asia into Turkestan
and China, and in parts of South-eastern Europe.

All this activity offers a close parallel to the work of the monastic
organizations in Northern and Central Europe. But Muslim
missionary activity was always peculiarly individual and unregu-
lated. The Sūfi movement was never fully co-ordinated with the
orthodox scholastic organization, but jealously maintained independence of, and even some degree of antagonism towards it. There
was no orthodox central authority to bring them together and to
assume the control and direction of Sūfi activities. True, there was
at one time the Caliphate. But the Caliphate was not a Papacy, and
from Umayyad times on the theologians and legists had resolutely
refused to concede to it any spiritual authority. The Caliphs were
the religious as well as secular heads of the Islamic community, in
that they embodied the supremacy of the Faith and the Sacred Law.
But an attempt by three Caliphs in the ninth century to define
orthodox dogma was decisively defeated, and the attempt was never
repeated.

Furthermore, independent rulers, while outwardly acknowledg-
ing the religious authority of the Caliphs, were quick to resent and
to suppress interference in the affairs of their kingdoms. Not
infrequently they held their Sūfi spiritual directors in higher esteem
than the orthodox scholars and legists, who for their part also found
themselves in a somewhat ambiguous relationship to the secular
power.

Since the tenth century the State had gradually diverged more and more from the path traced out by the Muslim theorists. It elaborated an ethic of its own, whose values were derived from the old imperial traditions of Asia and very far removed from the Islamic values. Against this inverted culture the Muslim legists waged an unceasing struggle, in the effort to reconvert the State into an embodiment of the principles of the Sacred Law. Later on, indeed, Muslim political theorists, accommodating themselves to the changed situation, began to distinguish Caliphate from Kingship, applying the former term in a new sense to denote any government which recognized and enforced the Sacred Law, as against a secular despotism which governed by arbitrary or natural law.

But while the conflict to maintain the Muslim ideals preserved the spiritual and intellectual life of Islam from stagnation, the legists were fighting on the whole a losing battle. The fault lay partly in themselves, that the more scrupulous were loth to hold any religious office under the Sultans and, in rejecting public service, left the field to their more time-serving and less scrupulous brethren. While the purity of their motives may be respected, their withdrawal weakened their power to combat effectively the vices which were taking firm root amongst the governing classes in every province of the Muslim world. The middle classes in general, on the other hand, accepted—if they did not always live up to—the Islamic ideal, and as time went on both they and the theologian-legists were more and more permeated by Sūfi influences. Thus one may say, with some little exaggeration, that in the Muslim world, concealed by common outward profession of Islam, there were two distinct societies living side by side and interacting to some extent but in their basic principles opposed to one another.

The evolution sketched above was greatly accelerated by the disasters which followed one another in Western Asia in the thirteenth and fourteenth centuries. A first invasion of heathen Mongols devastated the north-eastern provinces between 1220 and 1225. The second wave occupied Persia and Iraq, put an end to the historic Caliphate of Baghdad in 1258, and made the whole eastern Muslim world, except Egypt, Arabia, and Syria, tributary to the vast Mongol Empire. The remnants were saved by the military caste of Turkish and Kipchak 'slaves', the Mamlūks, who had seized the political power in Egypt. Under Mamlūk rule the old Arabic Muslim civilization continued for some two and a half centuries to flourish in the material arts (especially in architecture and metal-work), but with a gradual decay of spiritual and intellectual vigour.

Meanwhile, a revived and in some respects brilliant Persian Muslim civilization grew up in the Mongol dominions. It too excelled in architecture and the fine arts, including the art of minia-ture painting; spiritually it was rooted in Sūfism. In spite of two virulent 'Black Deaths' and the destructive campaigns of Timur (Tamerlane) in the fourteenth century, which reduced Persia itself to a state of extreme physical exhaustion, Persian culture moulded the intellectual life of the new Islamic empires that were growing up on either side—in Anatolia and the Balkans, and in India.

The expansion of the Ottoman Empire in Asia and North Africa and the establishment of the Mughal Empire in India in the sixteenth century brought the greater part of the Muslim world once more under the government of powerful and highly centralized civil States. A marked feature of both Empires was the strong emphasis laid on Muslim orthodoxy and the Sacred Law; Church and State were not indeed unified, since the military and higher civil polity was constructed on independent non-Islamic lines, but buttressed one another by a sort of concordat that endured into the nineteenth century.

Yet of the two channels of Muslim religious life the mystical was the broader and deeper. The seventeenth and early eighteenth cen-turies saw the apogee of the Sūfi brotherhoods. The greater orders spread a network of congregations from end to end of the Islamic world, while smaller local orders and sub-orders grouped the members of different classes and occupations into compact com-munities. Apart from this, Islamic culture in both Empires lived on the heritage of the past, preserving, but scarcely adding to, its intellectual patrimony. The primary task to which its representatives felt themselves called was not to expand, but rather to conserve, to unify, and to stabilize social life on Muslim standards. Within these limits, the measure of unity which they achieved and the social stability which they maintained was indeed remarkable.

To this unification there was one conspicuous exception. Early in the sixteenth century a new dynasty, supported by Turkish tribes from Azerbaijan, conquered Persia, revived the long-decaying Shi'ite heterodoxy, and established it as the religion of the Persian State. Through the long series of wars with the Ottomans, the Central-Asian Turks, and the Mughals, all of whom were Sunnis, Shi'ism became identified with Persian national feeling. The consequences of this double rift between Persia and its neighbours were serious for all. It broke the orthodox Muslim community into two separate halves between whom effective cultural communication, though not entirely cut off, was sporadic and small. And it forced Persia into a self-imposed political and religious isolation, which ultimately impoverished its spiritual and cultural life. Moreover, as its political strength declined, the Afghan tribesmen broke away in the eighteenth century to form an independent orthodox Sunni State.

The eighteenth century witnessed also the decline of Ottoman and Mughal military power. The Mughal State was undermined by a Hindu revolt under the Mahrattas, which led up to the British conquest. The Ottomans succeeded in reasserting their authority in their Asiatic territories in the first half of the nineteenth century, but only by the application of European techniques which gradually sapped the old Muslim society. When, as a result of the first World War, the Arab lands slipped from their grasp, they gave way to a new and secularized Turkish Republic in the smaller but more homogeneous Turkish lands in Anatolia and Eastern Thrace.

But the decay of Muslim political power did not carry with it a corresponding weakening in the forces of Islamic society. Church and State had long since become, as we have seen, separate entities, and it would almost seem that the decline of the latter injected a new vitality into the former. The evolution of Islam during the last two centuries will be treated in fuller detail in the final chapter of this book, and it remains only to add here a few words on its expansion in the outlying Muslim territories.

In North-West Africa the prevalence of tribalism amongst both Arabs and Berbers heavily handicapped cultural activities, and orthodoxy as well as the Sūfi orders were contaminated by the local cults of living saints ('marabouts'). But in Tunis and a few other towns something of the legacy of Spanish-Arabic culture was maintained, even when Tunisia and Algeria became piratical semi-dependencies of the Ottoman Empire. In Morocco also, under the Sultans (who preserved their independence until 1912), and even under some lesser chiefs in the Western Sahara, the traditional orthodox studies continued to be cultivated and were from time to time reinforced by influences transmitted from the East.

In West Africa Islam made little progress during the centuries that followed the decline of the medieval Mandingo negro empires. In the first half of the nineteenth century a succession of warring negro chieftains created ephemeral kingdoms by conquest among the pagan tribes. But a more enduring impress was and continues to be made by the missionary orders who followed in their wake and by peaceful propaganda succeeded to a large extent in mitigating the hostility aroused by their savagery. In East Africa there was little Muslim penetration into the interior in spite of ancient and flourishing settlements on the coast. The main cause of their failure was apparently the slave trade, since its suppression was followed by an outburst of missionary activity, conducted mainly by Swahilis. In South Africa Islam is represented chiefly by Malay and Indian immigrants.

In the Malay Archipelago itself Islam gained a footing in Sumatra and Java through traders in the thirteenth and fourteenth centuries, and gradually spread, partly by the exploits of military chieftains but more effectively through peaceful penetration, especially in Java. From Sumatra it was carried by colonists to the Malay Peninsula, and from Java to the Moluccas, and it has gained a more or less firm footing in all the islands eastwards to the Sulu Archipelago and Mindanao in the Philippines.

The spread of Islam in China is still shrouded in obscurity. The first extensive settlement of Muslims probably dates from the Mongol Empire in the thirteenth and fourteenth centuries. Under the Manchus their numbers greatly increased in spite of the hostility aroused by occasional (and sometimes formidable) Muslim risings, but it is impossible to reach at present even an approximate estimate of their strength.

The net result of this expansion over thirteen centuries is that Islam is today the dominant religion in a wide belt of territory which extends across North Africa and Western Asia up to the Pamirs and thence eastwards through Central Asia into China proper and southwards to Pakistan. Reduced in India to one-tenth of the population, it becomes predominant again in the Malay Peninsula and through the chain of the East Indies till it tapers away in the Philippines. On the western coast of the Indian Ocean it extends down a narrow strip of the African coast to Zanzibar and Tanganyika, with discontinuous groups continuing into the Union of South Africa. In Europe Muslim communities exist in most of the Balkan countries and in Southern Russia, and it is represented in both North and South America by small groups of immigrants from the Middle East.

Of all the great religions of the world, Islam embraced—prior to the expansion of Christian missionary activity in the nineteenth century—the widest variety of races. Originating amongst Arabs and other 'Semitic' peoples, it spread among Iranians, Caucasians, Mediterranean Whites, Slavs, Turks and Tatars, Chinese, Indians, Indonesians, Bantus, and West African Negroes. The largest contingent today are the Muslims of Pakistan and India, numbering some 120,000,000. After them come the Malays and Indonesians with some 110,000,000. The Arabs and Arabic-speaking communities run them close with about 30,000,000 Muslims in Western Asia, 40,000,000 in Egypt and the Eastern Sudan, and 32,000,000 of mixed Arab and Berber descent in the rest of North Africa. Persia has 25,000,000, Afghanistan about 18,000,000, and Turkey (where Islam, though disestablished, is still the religion of the people) 30,000,000. The size of the Muslim communities in the Asiatic territories of the U.S.S.R., in Chinese Turkestan, and in China proper is difficult to estimate, but they must number 40,000,000 at the least. The Muslims of Negro and East Africa can only be roughly estimated at 72,000,000. Finally, the Muslims in the Balkans and South Russia number some 3,000,000. In all, therefore, Islam may claim some 500,000,000 adherents, or about one-seventh of the total estimated population of the world.

2
Mohammed

ISLAM, IT used to be said, grew up in the full light of history. Within a single lifetime that light has grown steadily dimmer. Under critical examination the foundations of the old tradition have dissolved into enigmas and hypotheses. The Koran emerges so far unscathed, and the bare historical framework survives. But the gap between the bare facts and the tremendous results, between cause and effect, has to be filled up somehow. Consequently, there are almost as many theories about Mohammed as there are biographers. He has, for example, been portrayed as an epileptic, as a socialist agitator, as a proto-Mormon. All such extreme subjective views are generally repudiated by the main body of scholars, yet it remains almost impossible to avoid importing some subjective elements into any account of his life and work.

Mohammed suffered, on the one hand, like every other creative personality, the constraints of external circumstances, and on the other he broke a new channel through the ideas and conventions of his time and place. To study and elucidate this interplay between genius and its environment is the task of historical research. In the context of this book the study must be limited to his religious mission. But this is, indeed, the fundamental aspect of Mohammed. The one certain fact is that his impulse was religious through and through. From the beginning of his career as a preacher his outlook and his judgement of persons and events were dominated by his conceptions of God's government and purposes in the world of men.

Of his early life and circumstances little is known with certainty.

That he was born (the traditional date is A.D. 570) into a cadet branch of one of the leading families of Mecca, was left an orphan in early life and brought up by an uncle, engaged in the caravan trade, became commercial agent to a widow named Khadija, married her and had children (of whom four daughters survived)—all this is commonplace and gives no hint of future greatness. The anecdotal detail with which pious tradition delighted to fill out these bare outlines must be provisionally set aside. Of much greater importance is his social background. Mohammed was a citizen of no mean city. Nothing can be further from the reality than to picture him as a Bedouin, sharing the ideas and outlook of the Bedouin tribesmen.

Mecca at this time was no sleepy hollow, remote from the noise and bustle of the world. A busy and wealthy commercial town, almost monopolizing the entrepôt trade between the Indian Ocean and the Mediterranean, it recalls Palmyra without the flashy Greek veneer. Its citizens, while preserving a certain native Arab simplicity in their manners and institutions, had acquired a wide knowledge of men and cities in their intercourse, commercial and diplomatic, with Arab tribesmen and Roman officials. Amongst their leaders these experiences had stimulated intellectual faculties and moral qualities of prudence and self-restraint rare in Arabia. The moral predominance so acquired by the Meccans over the tribesmen was further strengthened by possession of a group of sanctuaries in and near the city. The impress of this exceptional background can be traced throughout Mohammed's career. Humanly speaking, Mohammed succeeded because he was a Meccan.

But there was a darker side to the prosperity of Mecca. It displayed the familiar evils of a wealthy commercial society, extremes of wealth and poverty, an underworld of slaves and hirelings, social class-barriers. It is clear from Mohammed's fervent denunciations of social injustice and fraud that this was one of the deep inner causes of his unsettlement. But the ferment within him did not break out in the preaching of social revolution; it was thrust instead into a religious channel and issued in a deep and unshakable conviction that he was called by God to proclaim to his fellow-citizens the old warning of the Semitic prophets: Repent, for the Judgement of God is at hand.

Everything that followed was the resultant of the clash between this conviction and the unbelief and resistance of one group after another. Mohammed was not at the outset the conscious preacher of a new religion. It was opposition and controversy with the Meccans that forced him on from stage to stage, as it was the later opposition in Medina that led to the final emergence of Islam as a new religious community with its distinctive faith and institutions.

The resistance of the Meccans appears to have been due not so much to their conservatism or even to religious disbelief (though they ridiculed Mohammed's doctrine of resurrection) as to political and economic causes. They were afraid of the effects that his preaching might have on their economic prosperity, and especially that his pure monotheism might injure the economic assets of their sanctuaries. In addition, they realized more quickly than Mohammed himself did that their acceptance of his teaching would introduce a new and formidable kind of political authority into their oligarchic community.

Against their self-interested opposition Mohammed struggled in vain. After ten years' labour at Mecca he had gathered only a small band of devoted adherents. A complete standstill followed. At this point he was driven to contemplate the necessity of a decisive and revolutionary step. He must break those sacred ties of kinship which had hitherto protected him, and transfer his mission to a new centre. His first essays brought nothing but vexation. But suddenly and unexpectedly the way opened before him. Two hundred miles north of Mecca, the city of Medina was suffering from a prolonged fratricidal war between rival Arab tribes. Exhausted, and fearing lest their weakness should be exploited by the Jewish tribes under their control, they besought Mohammed to come to Medina as arbitrator and peacemaker. With his habitual prudence he first exacted guarantees for the security of his own position and for the right of his followers to precede him to Medina. Negotiations were prolonged over one or two years; but at length, in the autumn of 622, Mohammed fled secretly from Mecca, escaped his pursuers, and established himself in his new base.

The Hijra is often regarded as marking a new era in the character and activities of Mohammed, but the sharp contrast which is generally drawn between the obscure and persecuted prophet of Mecca and the warrior theocrat of Medina is not historically justified. There was no break in Mohammed's own consciousness and conception of his office. Externally, the Islamic movement assumed a new shape and formed a definite community organized on political lines under a single chief. But this merely gave explicit form to what had hitherto been implicit. In the mind of Mohammed (as in the minds of his opponents) the new religious association had long been conceived of as a community organized on political lines, not as a church within a secular state. In his expositions of prophetic history this was an essential part of the Divine purpose in sending prophets. We need not look outside Arabia for the source of this conception, although if Mohammed had done so he would have found religion and state bound up together in all contemporary organizations, Persia, Byzantium, and Abyssinia.

The novelty, then, at Medina was that the religious community was translated from theory to practice. Even then, it was primarily not as a result of Mohammed's own efforts, since Medina had sought him, not he Medina. This was a clear proof for him and his followers of Divine support. All later developments in his preaching and in early Islamic conceptions derive naturally from the fact of the corporal existence of the community and the necessary (but not always easy) accommodation of the ideal to the stubborn facts and practical conditions of mundane life.

It remained now to establish it securely, but how? Mohammed had tried peaceful persuasion, and it had failed. The opposition of the Meccans had been founded on political and economic grounds; only through political and economic pressure could he break it down. Henceforward his political action revolved round two poles: the internal consolidation of the Muslim community and the coercion of Mecca. To put this second object down to mere desire for revenge is clearly insufficient. Even if he may have nourished at first some bitter feelings towards the city which had rejected him (and thereby, in his view, rejected the Divine message with which he was charged), Mecca soon resumed its place in the centre of his affections. Less than a year after the Hijra it was proclaimed the central shrine in the Islamic system, and thus became a kind of spiritual *irredenta*.

Mohammed's attitude towards Mecca was by this act elevated above the plane of personal feeling. Mecca was moreover the intellectual and political leader of Western Arabia; so long as Mecca remained hostile the Islamic community was in danger of extinction. More positively, Mohammed earnestly desired to enlist the talents of the Meccans in the service of Islam. Nowhere else in Western Arabia was there such intellectual grasp or such political capacity, though he realized as clearly that in depth of religious conviction Medina was the real spiritual centre of the new community.

At Medina he sat astride Mecca's vital trade route to the north. All his expeditions against the Bedouin tribes seem to be part of a master plan, elaborated with great skill and insight, to take advantage of this position and to blockade Mecca into surrendering. That this would provoke an armed conflict must have been foreseen, but the three major battles of Badr, Ohod, and the 'Ditch' fought in the second, third, and fifth years of the Hijra, have little more than episodic value, large as they may loom in Muslim tradition. It was essential for Mohammed's purposes that Mecca should come in eventually of its own volition, and his outstanding political genius is shown by the way in which Mecca was finally incorporated, after seven years of struggle, not as a beaten and resentful enemy but as a willing, if not enthusiastic partner. And when, two years later, Islam had to face its first great crisis on the death of Mohammed, Mecca was in fact foremost in lending its support to the re-establishment of the Islamic supremacy in Arabia.

Even in Mohammed's recourse to warfare against the tribes we must see more than a simple reflex of Arabian political and social conditions, although certainly something of that as well. Whatever worldly motives may from time to time have consciously or unconsciously influenced his course of action, his fundamental purpose remained exclusively religious. To the end, military and diplomatic action—for he never used the former if the latter sufficed, and after the surrender of Mecca purely military operations were discontinued —were regarded by him as an instrument for bringing moral and religious influences to bear on the proud and intractable tribesmen.

It must be added that every historical consideration which can be applied to the situation bears out the rightness of his view.

It would, however, be a serious mistake to imagine that Mohammed's interest and attention during these years were given up solely to politics and war. On the contrary, the centre of all his preoccupations was the training, educating, and disciplining of his community. They were to be the leaven to leaven the whole lump—for he had no illusions about the Arab character and realized that any genuine conversion of the majority could only be the end of a long process extending far beyond his own lifetime. His last two years were largely devoted to instilling into his former Meccan opponents something of the moral earnestness of his earlier followers and to fitting them to carry on his work after him. Consequently, the individuality of the Islamic community was progressively defined on parallel lines to its establishment as an independent political unit.

At the same time, whether deliberately guided by Mohammed in this direction or under the unconscious play of forces which swept him along in their current, the Islamic movement became, to an increasing degree, a focus of Arab feeling. In his later years, at least, Mohammed seems to have been aware of this tendency. It may have partially contributed to (and been confirmed by) his measures against the Jewish tribes. And whether or not the story be true that in 628 he sent summonses to the Roman Emperor, the Persian King of Kings, and other ruling princes, he was certainly contemplating some action against the Byzantine power in the north before his death in 632. The almost immediate launching of the first expeditions towards Syria by his successor Abu Bakr can hardly be explained otherwise. It is indeed quite possible that Mohammed's later change of attitude towards Christianity reflects his growing hostility to the Greeks and their Christian Arab allies, Orthodox or Monophysite.

When one turns from Mohammed's public life to his personality and his moral and social influence, it is not always easy to steer a straight course between the *odium theologicum* of most earlier Western critics and the unconvincing apologetic of modern Muslim writers. The study of the sources has not yet gone far enough to enable us to distinguish with confidence genuine early tradition from later accretions. For it must be confessed that the figure of

Mohammed has suffered greatly from the hodge-podge of trivialities fathered upon him by later generations of his followers. Yet through the mass of all-too-human detail there shines out unmistakably a largeness of humanity—sympathy for the weak, a gentleness that seldom turned to anger save when dishonour seemed to be done to God, something even of shyness in personal intercourse, and a glint of humour—all of which contrasts so strangely with the prevailing temper and spirit of his age and of his followers that it cannot be other than a reflection of the real man. During a Pilgrimage Abu Bakr started to beat a man for letting a camel stray; Mohammed 'began to smile and said "Just look at what this pilgrim is doing" '. A trivial story; but nothing perhaps illustrates better the gulf between Mohammed and the human material with which he had to deal than the fact that the narrator adds 'but he did not actually forbid him'.

It is at bottom the same incomprehension which leads critics to rely exclusively upon the Koran in their judgement of Mohammed. No doubt the Koran reflects in its basic religious attitudes the personality of the preacher; but the mistake lies in equating the preacher with the man. Mohammed seems to have been sharply aware of the distinction between legislation on the one hand and personal precept and example on the other. In laying down laws he took into account the conservatism and resistance of Arabian society and recognized just how far he could enforce the reform of its usages by decree. Thus the Koran sanctions, under legal regulation and safeguards, such practices as retaliation, but seldom fails to add in the same breath recommendations to temper the rigour of justice with mercy and the charity that comes from the realization of one's own need of forgiveness.

The most striking example is to be found in his legislation on divorce and family life. That his reforms enhanced the status of women in general by contrast with the anarchy of pre-Islamic Arabia is universally admitted. Yet the Koran explicitly maintains the superior right both of the father and of the husband, and legalizes polygamy up to four wives and repudiation under certain restrictions. Further than this Mohammed evidently could not go by the method of legislation, and even so it was not long before most of the rights accorded to women and of the restrictions imposed upon their guardians were substantially curtailed by the ingenuity of Muslim casuists.

The tradition on the other hand unanimously emphasizes his personal disapproval of repudiation as a thing 'odious in the sight of God'. His own family life at Medina and his numerous marriages have been the subject of much insinuating comment on the one side and of heated and disingenuous apology on the other. The traditions make no secret of the attraction which he felt towards women, or of the fact that it was combined with a peculiarly strict regard for the proprieties. But critics have tended to overlook the almost unfailing patience which he displayed even under provocation and the gentleness with which he attended to the griefs of all sorts of women and comforted them, even at times to the extent of revising his legislation.

For us it goes without saying that the hold which Mohammed gained over the wills and affections of his Companions were due to the influence of his personality. Without that they would have paid little heed to the claims of the Prophet. It was because of his moral qualities, not because of his religious teaching, that the men of Medina invoked his assistance. Ultimately, no doubt, even for the Companions, the two aspects of his life became indistinguishable, as they have remained for all Muslims of later generations.

It was natural, therefore, that as soon as the compelling personality of the man was withdrawn, veneration for the Prophet led almost at once to the enhancement of the story of his life by internal development and by elements introduced into it from without. At a later stage, when the social and ethical conceptions of Muslims had been refined under the influence of new literary and philosophical currents, the figure of the Prophet was continually readjusted to the new ideas and ideals. In a later chapter it will be seen how Sūfis fitted Mohammed into their mystical cosmology and system of saint-worship. By this time, idealization of the Prophet had passed from the field of ethics into something like a necessity of the spiritual life; but however far it went, Muslim thought never quite lost touch with the human figure of Mohammed ibn Abdullah, the man of Mecca.

3
The Koran

THE KORAN is the record of those formal utterances and discourses which Mohammed and his followers accepted as directly inspired. Muslim orthodoxy therefore regards them as the literal Word of God mediated through the angel Gabriel. They are quoted with the prefix 'God has said'; the phrase 'The Prophet said' is applied only to the sayings of Mohammed preserved in the Traditions. Mohammed's own belief, which is still held without question by his followers, was that these discourses were portions of a 'Heavenly Book' sent down to or upon him in an Arabic version, not as a whole, but in sections of manageable length and in relation to the circumstances of the moment.

In outward form the Koran is a book of some 300 pages, divided into 114 chapters, called sūras, arranged roughly in order of length, except for the short prayer which constitutes Sūra i. Sūra ii has 286 verses, Sūra iii 200, and so on, down to the final sūras, which have only three to five short verses. As the Medinian sūras are generally the longer ones the order is not chronological; and the difficulty of rearranging them in chronological order is increased by the fact that most of the Medinian and many of the Meccan sūras are composite, containing discourses or different periods bound up together. Apart from the relatively few allusions to exactly dated historical events, the principal evidences are supplied by general criteria of style and content.

In the earliest period of his preaching Mohammed's utterances were delivered in a sinewy oracular style cast into short rhymed

phrases, often obscure and sometimes preceded by one or more
formal oaths. This style is admittedly that of the ancient *kāhins* or
Arabian oracle-mongers, and it is not surprising that Mohammed's
opponents should have charged him with being just another such
kāhin. For this and other reasons his style gradually loosened out
into a simpler but still rhetorical prose; and as social denunciations
and eschatological visions passed into historical narrative, and that
in turn at Medina into legislation and topical addresses, little was
left of its original stylistic features but a loose rhyme or assonance
marking the end of each verse, now anything from ten to sixty
words long.

Carlyle's dictum on the Koran: 'It is as toilsome reading as I
ever undertook, a wearisome, confused jumble, crude, incondite.
Nothing but a sense of duty could carry any European through the
Koran' puts succinctly what must indeed be the first impression of
any reader. But years of close study confirm his further judgement
that in it 'there is a merit quite other than the literary one. If a book
come from the heart, it will contrive to reach other hearts; all art
and authorcraft are of small account to that.' Though, to be sure,
the question of literary merit is one not to be judged on *a priori*
grounds but in relation to the genius of the Arabic language; and
no man in fifteen hundred years has ever played on that deep-toned
instrument with such power, such boldness, and such range of
emotional effect as Mohammed did.

In trying to trace the sources and development of the religious
ideas expounded in the Koran (a question, be it remembered, not
only meaningless but blasphemous in Muslim eyes), we are still confronted with many unsolved problems. Earlier scholars postulated a
Jewish source with some Christian additions. More recent research
has conclusively proved that the main external influences (including
the Old Testament materials) can be traced back to Syriac
Christianity.

It is now well known that there were organized Jewish and
Christian churches amongst the settled communities in the north,
the south, and the east of Arabia. The Arab town of Hīra on the
Euphrates was the seat of a Nestorian bishopric which almost certainly conducted some kind of missionary activity in Arabia, and

there are many references in old Arabic poetry to hermits living in lonely cells in the wilderness. In the Yemen a Jewish or Judaizing movement supported by the local dynasty was overthrown by the Yemenite Christians with Abyssinian aid in A.D. 525. In view of the close commercial relations between Mecca and the Yemen it would be natural to assume that some religious ideas were carried to Mecca with the caravans of spices and woven stuffs, and there are details of vocabulary in the Koran which give colour to this assumption.

From the Koran itself it is clear that monotheistic ideas were familiar in Western Arabia. The existence of a supreme God, Allah, is assumed as an axiom common to Mohammed and his opponents. The Koran never argues the point; what it does argue is that He is the one and only God. *Lā ilāha illa'llāh*, 'there is no god but Allah'.

But it is more doubtful whether this is to be regarded as the direct deposit of Christian or Jewish teaching. In the Koran it is connected with a different tradition altogether, an obscure Arabian tradition represented by the so-called *hanīfs*, pre-Islamic Arab monotheists whose very name shows that the Syrians regarded them as non-Christians (Syriac *hanpā*, 'heathen'). Mohammed glories in the name and attaches it as a distinctive epithet to Abraham, who was 'neither Jew nor Christian'. There is even a suggestion in an early variant reading of a Koranic verse (iii, v. 17) that at one time *Hanīfiyya* was used to denote the doctrine preached by Mohammed and was only later replaced by *Islām*.

A further trace of this native North-Arabian prophetic tradition is found in the early passages of the Koran which refer to or recount the missions of former prophets. In these narratives certain obscure Arabian figures—Hūd, Shu'aib and others—take a place at least as prominent as the prophets of the Old Testament. The earliest references assume that the stories of these prophets were familiar to Mohammed's hearers, and indeed one or two of them are mentioned in pre-Islamic verses.

But while granting this native monotheistic tradition as an integral element in Mohammed's background or ideas, the doctrine which most powerfully gripped him (and which, through him, was most vividly impressed upon the mind of Islam in all later ages) was the doctrine of the Last Judgement. This was certainly not derived from the Arabian tradition, but from Christian sources. The profound disbelief and scornful sarcasms with which it was received by his Meccan fellow-citizens show that it was a wholly unfamiliar idea to them. On the other hand, not only the ideas expressed by Mohammed about the resurrection of the physical body and the future life, but also many of the details about the process of the Judgement and even the pictorial presentation of the joys of Paradise and torments of Hell, as well as several of the special technical terms employed in the Koran, are closely paralleled in the writings of the Syriac Christian fathers and monks.

Whatever may have been the channels through which these ideas reached Mohammed, the fear of God's 'wrath to come' dominated his thought throughout his later life. It was for him not only, nor even chiefly, a weapon with which to threaten his opponents, but the incentive to piety and good works of every kind. The characteristic sign of the Believer is ever-present fear of God, and its opposite is 'heedlessness' or 'frivolity'. This antithesis was never absent from Mohammed's mind, and it forms the recurrent motive of early Muslim asceticism, which in this certainly reflected the central element in his teaching. That God is the omnipotent master and man His creature who is ever in danger of incurring His wrath —this is the basis of all Muslim theology and ethics. Forgiveness is only to be attained by the grace of God; man cannot win it for himself by merit; but to be worthy to attain it requires of man unrelenting self-control and the service of God by means of good works and especially by prayer and alms-giving.

Prophets are not theologians, and it could scarcely be demanded that Mohammed's expositions of this doctrine should have been theologically precise and rigid. The Koran sways between the conceptions of predestination and freewill, according to whether the relevant verses are addressed to the unheeding multitude or to the group of Believers. The carelessness of the world was a source of continued bewilderment to Mohammed, as to most religious minds, and seemed to be explicable only as the act of God; but some less deterministic formulation was needed to account for the merit attached to the performance of ethical and religious duties and to encourage the Believers to persevere in them.

For Mohammed did not preach solely a doctrine of damnation by an omnipotent and jealous God. Combined with this was a gospel of hope. As the little community grew in numbers God's mercy was stressed again and again. At one time, indeed, Mohammed adopted a name for God which pre-Islamic inscriptions show to have been current in Arabia—*ar-Rahmān*, 'The Compassionate One'; and this term survived in the formula prefixed to every sūra of the Koran (and presumably to each of Mohammed's discourses), *bismi'llāh ir-rahmān ir-rahīm*, 'In the Name of God, the Compassionate One, the Merciful'.

Meanwhile the controversy with his Meccan opponents was forcing him to develop the content of his preaching. As they remained impervious to his claims to have been sent to warn them against God's wrath on the Day of Judgement and to his appeals to repent of their errors and evil deeds, his tone became more argumentative. In ever-increasing detail he expanded his exposition of the evidences in nature for the existence and power of God and of the missions of earlier prophets. It was now not only the final retribution of the Judgement Day that he stressed, but also the prospect of some awful calamity in the present life in punishment for their rejection of his warning. He recalled again and again the catastrophes that had overtaken the Egyptians, the 'people of Lot', the 'people of Noah', and those Arabian tribes who had rejected his predecessors. New prophetic narratives—the stories of Joseph and John the Baptist, the first draft of the story of Jesus, stories of David and Solomon, of the 'Two-horned', the Seven Sleepers, and other figures from apocryphal tradition and the Alexander-legend—were added for homiletic purposes or to demonstrate the supernatural origin of his knowledge.

But the Meccans still demanded of him a miracle, and with remarkable boldness and self-confidence Mohammed appealed as the supreme confirmation of his mission to the Koran itself. Like all Arabs they were connoisseurs of language and rhetoric. Well then, if the Koran were his own composition other men could rival it. Let them produce ten verses like it. If they could not (and it is obvious that they could not), then let them accept the Koran as an outstanding evidential miracle.

During the later years at Mecca, years on the whole of disappoint-ment and apparent stagnation, there was little fresh stimulus to widen the range of Mohammed's preaching. In the sūras of this period old themes are repeated again and again; the general tone is sombre, and there are passages of anxious and heart-searching medita-tion. Yet these were years of great importance for the development of the Islamic community. In the face of growing hostility, religious emotion, pent between narrow walls, ground a channel down to the very heart. Persecutions and social obstacles, while they weeded out the weaker converts, hardened that core of moral earnestness which proved to be at once the driving force and the sheet-anchor of the Islamic movement after the death of the Prophet.

It must also be assumed that during this period the ritual of prayer was being stabilized. The traditions frequently refer to the prayers, both public and private, of Mohammed and his followers. But the Meccan sūras mention only morning and evening prayers and private prayer during the night; indeed, the Koran nowhere explicitly prescribes the five daily prayers nor the ritual of prostra-tion. Nor, of course, were there as yet any precise legal or social prescriptions. Although the giving of alms, for example, is repeatedly stressed, the recommendation is formulated in terms of ethical duty as a means of self-purification, not in terms of an institution. And this is characteristic of the general tone of the Meccan sūras.

At Medina all this was changed. The existence of the new com-munity called for the promulgation of many rules of law and of social order as well as for the expansion of his ethical teaching. But the change was gradual. Mohammed's first 'legislative' enactment, the document in which he laid down the socio-political bases of the joint Medinian community, is not to be found in the Koran at all. That it was promulgated not as a revelation but on his own initiative throws some light on the distinction which he himself (and presum-ably his followers also) drew between revelation and personal action. An even more striking instance is furnished by his address at the 'Farewell Pilgrimage', when he visited Mecca for the last time; for this too, in spite of its religious content and the solemnity of the occasion, is not in the Koran.

These examples should make us pause before accepting the often-expressed view that Mohammed deliberately used 'revelation' as a device for imposing his will upon the community or for solving the problems with which he was called upon to deal. Certainly the large number of passages in the Medinian sūras which relate to trifling incidents and to political and domestic matters must of themselves suggest this to the critic. Yet amongst the most genuine traditions there are many which relate to very much the same kind of incidents and many striking homilies. Whatever the psychological explanation may be, it is difficult to resist the conclusion that the term 'revelation' was confined to those utterances which were not consciously produced and controlled by the Prophet and seemed to him to have been put into his mouth from without.

During the first year at Medina, Mohammed adopted several Jewish practices for the use of the Muslim community, such as the *āshūrā* fast on the tenth day of the first month (corresponding to the Day of Atonement), the institution of a midday prayer, and facing towards Jerusalem during prayer. But it was not long before he found himself involved in bitter controversy and conflict with the Jewish tribes. Fragments of the disputes preserved in the Koran indicate clearly enough their general character. The Jews obviously refused to acknowledge Mohammed's claim to prophethood and to 'confirm the Tōrah', and from contradiction passed to mockery; while he, confident of his divine mission, charged them with falsifying their scriptures and concealing their true contents. To their criticisms of his prophetic narratives he replied at first with convincing simplicity 'Are ye more knowing than God?' (Sūra ii, v. 134). But the rift widened, and from attempts at persuasion the Koran turns to upbraiding, sarcastic reproof, and finally denunciation and threats—in all (strangely enough) reproducing many themes of the old anti-Jewish polemic of the early Christian writers.

Although one of the charges repeatedly pressed against the Jews is their rejection of 'the Messiah Jesus son of Mary', the Koran includes the Christians also in the scope of its polemic. 'The Jews say the Christians have nothing to stand on, and the Christians say the Jews have nothing to stand on, and yet they both read the Book' (Sūra ii, v. 107). More especially the doctrine of the divine Sonship of Jesus is emphatically repudiated, in terms which betray the crassly anthropomorphic form in which it had been presented or presented itself to the Arabs. An early Meccan sūra (cxii), probably directed originally against the conception of the three Meccan goddesses as 'daughters of Allah', was evidently applicable also to the Christian doctrine of the Trinity: 'Say, He is God, One[1]—God the Eternal —He hath not begotten nor was He begotten—And there is none equal to Him.' But the Virgin Birth and the Immaculate Conception are reasserted; on the other hand, the crucifixion of Jesus is declared to be a Jewish calumny and denied, another in his semblance having been crucified in his place and Jesus himself translated. It is evident, in fact, throughout the Koran that Mohammed had no direct knowledge of Christian doctrine.

The background of this polemic against Christianity is obscure, since it is apparently contemporary with several friendly references to Christians, and it antedates the conflict with the Christianized tribes of the north-west. It was no doubt implicit in Mohammed's teaching from the outset, but may have been brought out by rivalry with the religious reform movement which was growing up simultaneously under Nestorian influence in the oases of Eastern Nejd, then called Yemāma. It was not until the year after Mohammed's death, however, that the two movements were to engage in a life-or-death struggle.

However that may be, the consequence was to make clear to Mohammed what we may call the historical theory of Islam. Since Judaism was claimed as the religion of Moses and Christianity as the religion of Jesus, he went back behind both to the figure of Abraham 'the *Hanif*'. He, being neither Jew nor Christian, fitted into Mohammed's conception of a primitive undistorted monotheism, constantly revived by a succession of Prophets, of whom he himself, the last, was the true heir of Abraham and purifier of the errors of both the Jews and the Christians. It is possible that this too was a legacy of that indigenous Arabian prophetic tradition of which only vague suggestions have survived to us.

Moreover, through Ishmael, Abraham was already associated by

---

[1] Or, as most Muslim exegetes prefer, 'Say, God is One.' The word usually rendered 'Eternal' is also variously interpreted.

the scriptural religions with the Arabs, and (since the earliest Medinian sūra speaks of the 'standing-place of Abraham' at Mecca as a well-known site) it would seem that Abraham and Ishmael were already traditionally regarded as the founders of its sanctuary, the Kaaba. Thus Islam appeared, not as a new religion, but as a revival of pure Abrahamic monotheism, purified at once of the accretions of Judaism and Christianity and superseding them as the final revelation.

But this is not to say that Islam became thereby a specifically Arabian form of monotheism. As will be seen in the next chapter, the one definitely Arabian institution retained in it is the Pilgrimage to Mecca, but by the reinterpretation of its ceremonies the Pilgrimage was given an ethical significance altogether foreign to its original Arabian character. Thus Islam, although a religion physically centred on Mecca, is not an Arabian religion, nor even an Arabian adaptation of Judaic and Christian monotheism, if by that is implied a lowering of the existing standards of Judaism and Syriac Christianity to a supposedly lower Arabian mentality. On the contrary, the whole function of Islam was to raise both Arabian and non-Arabian religious conceptions and ethical standards to the levels set by the preaching of the earlier Prophets.

Consequently, although polemic against the Jews, the luke-warm or time-serving elements in Medina (whom the Koran usually designates as 'the slinkers' or 'the sick-hearted'), and the fickle Bedouin tribesmen occupies a considerable portion of the Medinian sūras, it is subordinate to the inculcation of religious, ethical, and social duties. Since most of these will be considered in the next chapter, it will be enough here to try to sum up in a few words their general character.

Mohammed's system is rigid, positive, and emphatic. The rigidity, the special emphasis upon the compulsory performance of legal and religious duties, the demand for unquestioning obedience, can be explained largely as a reaction against the social and spiritual anarchy of Arabia. These Arabs, rebellious to all external control and devoid of self-discipline, must needs have the yoke fastened tightly upon their necks, or it would stand no chance of staying on at all. To 'go Arab', to sink back into the spiritual laxity of the tribesmen, was in

Mohammed's eyes backsliding into paganism, and he tried to keep his tribal converts as far as possible under his direct observation. There is a reality in the suggestion that the ceremonial bowings and prostrations in unison of the daily prayers were a means of physical as well as of spiritual discipline.

On the other side, and in reaction from the asceticism and tendency to withdraw from the world which was so marked a feature of Eastern Christianity, Mohammed from the first set his community squarely in the midst of the world. His often-quoted phrase 'No monkery in Islam' implies not only no professional cenobitism, but that the scene of religious activity in Islam is the life of men in the widest sense. All social activities were to be included within its purview and to be penetrated by its spirit. But this carried with it dangerous consequences. The inescapable impact of the outer world upon the religious ideals of Islam began even in the lifetime of the Prophet and among his closest Companions. It was hastened on and intensified by the vast territorial conquests of the next few years, and came to a head in civil war and the establishment of the Umayyad Caliphate at Damascus only twenty-eight years after his death. But it was this very capitulation to the world that proved to be the means of spiritual recovery for Islam. In the abandoned and now remote ancient capital of Medina, the living tradition of Mohammed survived, developed, and gained strength to resist and to overcome—to an extent which at first seemed impossible—the perils which too rapid and too sweeping a worldly success had brought in its train.

Whether the Koran was written down in full during Mohammed's lifetime is a question on which there are conflicting traditions. The generally received account describes its first compilation a few years after his death from 'scraps of parchment and leather, tablets of stone, ribs of palm branches, camels' shoulder-blades and ribs, pieces of board and the breasts of men'. To this, probably, is to be ascribed much of the unevenness and the rough jointing which characterize the present composition of the longer sūras. It is certain that, alongside these written materials, several of the Companions of the Prophet preserved by heart and transmitted versions with numerous small variants, and that the third Caliph, Othman, had an authoritative text prepared at Medina, copies of which were sent to the chief cities.

These copies, however, were written in the very defective early Arabian script, which needed to be supplemented by the trained memories of the thousands of 'reciters'. To meet this difficulty, improvements and refinements of orthography were gradually introduced into the old manuscripts. By the end of the first century the text as we now have it had been stabilized in all but a few details. Although in this process it was adjusted to the standard pronunciation, from which Mohammed's Meccan speech had differed in some small particulars, it seems reasonably well established that no material changes were introduced and that the original form and contents of Mohammed's discourses were preserved with scrupulous precision.

Yet so many minor variations in reading and punctuation still survived that ultimately the problem had to be met by a characteristic Muslim compromise, such as we shall meet again. First ten and then seven famous 'reciters' were recognized as authoritative teachers and all their 'readings' were accepted as orthodox. Although the learned claimed the right to accept the readings of other teachers, for all public purposes readings according to the text of one or other of the Seven only were adopted. In course of time several of these also dropped out of use, but it is only in the present century (as a result of the dissemination of printed and lithographed copies of the Koran from Constantinople and Cairo) that a single reading has acquired almost universal currency in the Muslim world.

In public recitation the Koran is intoned or chanted in slow melodic phrases, the correct art of which is taught as part of the normal academic course at Muslim religious seminaries. A specimen will be found in E. W. Lane's *Modern Egyptians*. In medieval times we hear of choirs of reciters. This practice has died out, but the services of professional chanters are still in great demand for both public and private occasions.

As in the case of all sacred books, the need was soon felt for some guidance in the interpretation and exegesis of the Koran. From the earliest days the transmission of the text was accompanied by oral glosses on points of language or interpretation. The glosses increased very greatly in number and complexity during the first two or three centuries, in consequence of the rise of theological and legal schools, of sectarian controversy, and of a great mass of popular tradition amplifying or claiming to explain the personal allusions and eschatological descriptions in the text. About the end of the third century the first collection and critical study of these materials was made by the theologian and historian al-Tabari (d. 923). His vast work, in thirty volumes, is a monument of scholarly piety, unequalled in his time or of its kind. It laid the foundations upon which later scholars built their more specialized commentaries, many of them with excellences of their own, such as that of the grammarian al-Zamakhshari (d. 1143). The philosopher al-Rāzi (d. 1209), using a different system of analysis and in more subjective fashion, summed up the exegetical discussions of the three centuries after al-Tabari. A century later, al-Baidāwi (d. 1286) brought together the various deposits of philological, theological, legal, and textual exegesis in a compendious commentary which has remained the standard work down to the present day. Modern orthodox interpretation stands on his shoulders, and so do all the European translations.

The Shi'ite interpretations are included in the commentaries of al-Tabarsi (d. 1153) and the voluminous later works of the Shi'ite writers of Persia.

4
Doctrine and Ritual in the Koran

ALTHOUGH IT would be vain to look in the Koran for a systematic exposition of Muslim beliefs or ritual, yet there emerges from it, taken as a whole, a consistent body of doctrine and of practical obligations. These have remained in all ages the core and inspiration of the Muslim religious life, and as such will be summarized in this chapter, leaving to subsequent chapters the later refinements of Muslim theology and practice.

Rather surprisingly, the famous *shahāda* or profession of faith: *lā ilāha illa'llāh muhammadun rasūlu'llāh*, 'There is but one God, Mohammed is the Apostle of God', is not found in this composite form anywhere in the Koran, but its two halves occur separately. What may be taken, however, as the outline of a *credo*—and often is so taken by Muslims—is given in Sūra iv, v. 135:

O ye who believe, believe in God and His Apostle and the Book which He hath sent down to His Apostle and the Scripture which He hath sent down formerly. Whosoever denieth God and His Angels and His Books and His Apostles and the Last Day hath strayed far from the Truth.

(i) *God*. The Arabic word *Allāh* is a shortened form of *al-ilāh*, '*The* god'. Both the concepts of a supreme God and the Arabic term have been shown to be familiar to the Arabs in Mohammed's time. What Mohammed did was to give a new and fuller content to the concept, to purify it from the elements of polytheism which still clustered round it, and to substitute for acceptance of a vague and distant figure belief in an intensely real, if transcendent, Being,

Creator and Sustainer of the universe, the all-knowing and all power-ful Arbiter of good and evil, and final Judge of all men.

To give even in outline all the teaching about God which is explicit or implicit in the Koran would be impossible here. Much of it is expressed in the form of epithets and adjectives, such as Hearer, Seer, Bestower, Reckoner, Pardoner, Keeper, Guide, from which Muslims have put together the ninety-nine 'most beautiful names' of God. But occasionally there are longer passages of exposition, the most impressive of which, in its sustained eloquence, is the famous Throne-verse (Sūra ii, v. 256):

God—there is no god but He, the Living, the Self-subsistent. Slumber seizeth Him not, neither sleep. To Him belongeth whatsoever is in the Heavens and whatsoever is in the Earth. Who is there that shall inter-cede with Him save by His Will? He knoweth what is present with men and what shall befall them, and nought of His knowledge do they com-prehend, save what He willeth. His Throne is wide as the Heavens and the Earth, and the keeping of them wearieth Him not. And He is the High, the Mighty One.

For Mohammed the essential element of true belief was an un-compromising monotheism. At Mecca he rejected the pretension that the goddesses worshipped by the Arabs were 'daughters of Allah', as later on he rejected the worship of Jesus and of Mary as 'lords' and upbraided the Jews for calling their religious teachers by the title of *rabbi* ('my lord'). True belief demands *ikhlās*, the giving of one's whole and unmixed allegiance to God, and its opposite is *shirk* the ascribing of partners to God and the worship of any creature. This is the one unforgivable sin: 'Verily God for-giveth not the giving of partners to Him; other than this will He forgive to whom He pleaseth, but whosoever giveth a partner to God hath conceived a monstrous sin' (iv, v. 51).

God exists from all eternity to all eternity. He is the only reality: 'Call not on any other god but Allah; there is no god but He. Every-thing shall perish except His Face.[1] To Him belongeth the rule and to Him shall ye be brought back for judgement' (xxviii, v. 88). All

[1] 'Face' is the term which in the Koran corresponds to *persona* or 'being'.

else from the Seven Heavens downwards comes into existence by His Will and at His creative Word 'Be!' He alone gives life and death, His Decree is inescapable, and all things are determined and disposed by His foreknowledge, pictorially expressed as written on a 'Preserved Tablet'. Men are His Creatures, *'ibād* (a plural of *'abd*, 'slave', already employed as a technical religious term by the Arab Christians), and must submit their wills to His ways, however mysterious. 'Peradventure ye may dislike some thing, yet God setteth in it abundant good' (iv, v. 18). He 'misleads whom He will and guides whom He will' (lxxiv, v. 34). Man must live in constant fear and awe of Him, and always be on his guard against Him (such is the idiomatic meaning of the term for 'fearing God' which runs through the Koran from cover to cover), yet he is bidden to adore Him, to magnify and praise Him, and ever to commemorate His Name.

For alongside the terrible and majestic aspects of God as Creator, Supreme Power, Judge, and Avenger, the Koran stresses also His bounty and loving-kindness. He is not only 'the Compassionate One, the Merciful', but also the Protector, the Provider, the Pardoner, the Clement, ever ready to turn to the repentant sinner. He is the Subtle, Who is 'closer to man than his own neck-vein' (l, v. 15), 'the First and the Last, the Manifest and the Hidden' (lvii, v. 3). And finally the mystical indwelling of God in His universe is suggested in the parable of the 'Light-verse' (xxiv, v. 35):

God is the Light of the Heavens and of the Earth. The similitude of His Light is as it were a niche wherein is a lamp, the lamp within a glass, the glass as though it were a pearly star. It is lit from a blessed Tree, an olive-tree neither of the East nor of the West, the oil whereof were like to shine even though no fire were applied to it; Light upon Light; God guideth to His Light whom He will.

(ii) *Angels*. In the imagery of the Koran the angels are represented generally as God's messengers. They are, like men, His creatures and servants and worship Him continually; they bear up His throne, descend with His Decrees on the Night of Power, record men's actions, receive their souls when they die, and witness for or against them at the Last Judgement, and guard the gates of Hell.

At the battle of Badr they assisted the Muslims against the vastly superior forces of the Meccans.

Although the term Archangels is not found in the Koran, the idea seems to be implied in the mention of the Angel of Death, who is set in authority over men (xxxii, v. 11), and of Michael alongside Gabriel in one verse (ii, v. 92). But it is above all Gabriel who is God's chief messenger; and it is certain that the early Muslims identified Gabriel with that 'illustrious messenger, lord of power' who communicated the Koran to Mohammed (lxxxi, vv. 19–21), and again with the 'Holy Spirit' who announced the birth of Jesus to the Virgin Mary and is said in three passages to have 'strengthened' Jesus.

With the doctrine of angels goes also the doctrine of devils, although the devils are represented as rebellious *jinn* rather than fallen angels. The *jinn* are, like men, created, but of fire instead of earth; there are believers and infidels amongst them, and the unbelievers will be judged with men and condemned to Hell. The rebellious *jinn* are called *shaitāns*; they lead men astray, oppose the Prophets, and try to overhear what is discussed in Heaven but are driven off by shooting stars. They teach men sorcery, and were made subject to Solomon, for whom they lived and built.

The leader of these evil spirits is called 'the Shaitān' or Iblīs. His fall from a place among the angels was due to his refusal to worship Adam on God's command; for this he was accursed, but respited till the Day of Resurrection and given authority over those of mankind who should be seduced by him.

(iii) *Books and Apostles.* The doctrine of Apostles is, as the *shahāda* shows, next to the Unity of God the central doctrine of the Koran. At all times and to all peoples, including the *jinn*, God has sent messengers or prophets to preach the unity of God and to warn men of the Judgement. Most, if not all, were rejected and persecuted by the majority of their fellow-citizens, who were subsequently visited by a terrible punishment. They were not workers of miracles, except when God endowed them with special powers as 'signs'. Muslims are required to believe in them all without distinction, although only a few are mentioned by name, or their histories related, in the Koran. Several received special endowments and rank above others, particularly Adam, Noah, the house of Abraham, Moses, and Jesus. The last or 'Seal' of the Prophets is Mohammed, who is God's Apostle to all mankind.

Altogether, twenty-eight Prophets are mentioned in the Koran. Of these, four (if Luqmān be included) are Arabian, eighteen are Old Testament figures, three (Zechariah, John the Baptist, and Jesus) are of the New Testament, and two are personages denoted by epithets—one being Dhu'l-Qarnain, 'The two-horned', commonly identified with the hero of the Alexander-legend. The prophetic narratives are almost all contained in Meccan passages, and in the case of the Biblical figures they correspond, with many variations, to the Biblical narratives. The story of Joseph occupies the whole of Sūra xii, and Sura xviii contains three independent stories, those of the Seven Sleepers, of the meeting of Moses with 'one of Our servants' (identified by Muslim tradition with the wandering saint al-Khidr), and of Dhu'l-Qarnain and the building of the wall of Gog and Magog. In the story of Jesus, which is found both in a Meccan and in a Medinian version, particular stress is laid on the Virgin Birth, his miracles, and the denial of his divinity or claim to divinity. The crucifixion is rejected as a Jewish fable, another in his semblance having been crucified in his stead.

The doctrine preached by all the Prophets is essentially one and the same, although in matters of detail there has been a gradual evolution in their messages towards the final and perfect revelation. These stages are represented also by the various 'books' or scriptures granted to several of the major Prophets. Several earlier scriptures are referred to anonymously, but four are singled out by name. To Moses was given by Divine inspiration the *Tawrāh*, the Jewish *Tōrah*, corresponding to the Pentateuch; to David the *Zabūr*, identified with the Psalms by a verbal quotation of Psalm xxxvii, v. 29 in Sūra xxi, v. 105; to Jesus the *Injīl*, the Evangel or Gospel; and to Mohammed the *Qur'ān* or Recital. All these scriptures were written revelations, and all alike are to be believed and accepted, since they all confirm one another and the Koran in particular not only confirms earlier scriptures, but, as the final revelation, clears up all uncertainties and is the repository of perfect Truth.

Furthermore, it is declared that the coming of Mohammed was

foretold by Jesus under the name of Ahmad, and that his name is specifically recorded in the *Tawrāh* and *Injīl* as the 'Prophet of the Gentiles' (*an-nabī al-ummī*, interpreted by later orthodoxy as 'the unlettered Prophet'). Nevertheless, the Jews (and perhaps, by implication, the Christians also) seek to conceal the witness of their scriptures and are guilty of misquoting and even of wilfully perverting them.

As for Mohammed himself, the Koran repeatedly disclaims on his behalf anything that savours of the superhuman. He is but a mortal man, commissioned with the sole duty of conveying God's warning and message of salvation. He has no knowledge beyond what is revealed to him, and has been granted no miraculous powers. He is commanded to seek pardon for his faults and to be patient under adversity. Yet he is a noble pattern to those who hope in God, his decisions must be accepted in matters of faith and conduct, belief in his revelation and obedience to him are necessary to salvation.

(iv) *The Last Day*. The place occupied by the Last Judgement in the mind of Mohammed and the imagination of his immediate followers has been indicated already in the previous chapter. It is presented always as a cataclysmic event, coming suddenly at a time known only to God. The Trumpet will be sounded, the heavens shall be split asunder and the mountains ground to dust, the graves will open, and men and *jinn* will be called to account. Each man's guardian angels will bear witness to his record, his deeds will be weighed in the Balance, and his book will be placed in his hand, the right hand of the blessed, the left hand of the damned.

Then the blessed, the godfearing men and women, the humble and charitable, the forgiving, those who have suffered and been persecuted for God's sake, those who have fought in the way of God, shall be summoned to enter the Garden of Paradise, the Abode of Peace, the abiding mansion, where they shall dwell for ever by flowing rivers, praising God, reclining on silken couches, enjoying heavenly food and drink and the company of dark-eyed maidens and wives of perfect purity, and yet greater bliss which no soul knoweth.

But the covetous, the unbelieving, the worshippers of gods other than Allah, shall be cast into the Fire, to abide therein for ever, with no release from its torments, fed with boiling water and the fruit of the *zaqqūm*, resembling the head of *shaitāns* and like molten brass in the belly. No description can indeed convey the terror of the Koranic portrayal of Hell, backed up as it is by the sombre asservation 'Verily I shall fill Hell with *jinn* and men altogether', or the horror of the day 'when We shall say to Hell "Art thou filled?" and Hell shall answer "Are there yet more?" ' (l, v. 29).

Yet this presentation of the awful reckoning is lightened by repeated assurances of the Divine Mercy and by hints of the power of intercession which God will grant to those whom He pleases, save on behalf of the evildoers in Hell. In no passage of the Koran, however, is the power of intercession specifically attributed to Mohammed, nor any suggestion that the profession of Islam in itself is a sure passport to Paradise. Apart from martyrs for the Faith, the only promise of Paradise is made to 'those who repent and believe and are righteous in act'.

Islamic orthodoxy has, accordingly, always coupled faith with works, and in particular with those 'acts of devotion' (*'ibādāt*) which are enjoined on Believers in the Koran.

(v) *Prayer.* The observance of the ritual prayers (*salāh*) is repeatedly emphasized as one of the essential religious duties. Although neither the ceremonies nor the five set times of prayer are precisely stated in the Koran, it is certain that they were well established before Mohammed's death. Each consists of a fixed number of 'bowings' (called *rak'ah*), the 'bowing' itself consisting of seven movements with their appropriate recitations: (1) the recitation of the phrase *Allāhu akbar*, 'God is most Great', with the hands open on each side of the face; (2) the recitation of the *Fātihah* or opening *sūra* of the Koran, followed by another passage or passages, while standing upright; (3) bowing from the hips; (4) straightening up; (5) gliding to the knees and a first prostration with face to the ground; (6) sitting back on the haunches; (7) a second prostration. The second and later 'bowings' begin with the second of these movements, and at the end of each pair of 'bowings' and the conclusion of the whole prayer the worshipper recites the *shahāda* and the ritual salutations.

The set times are at daybreak (2 *rak'ahs*), noon (4 *rak'ahs*), midafternoon (4 *rak'ahs*), after sunset (3 *rak'ahs*), and in the early part of the night (4 *rak'ahs*). At these times prayers should be said and the ritual observed by every Believer wherever he may be; but by preference they should be performed congregationally in a mosque (*masjid*, 'place of prostration') under the leadership of an *imām*, a man who, standing in front of the lines of worshippers, sets the timing of each movement. It seems that at Medina women joined in the congregational prayers, standing in rows behind the men. The *imām* and the worshippers face towards the *qibla*, the prescribed 'direction', which was defined in an early Medinian verse as the Sacred Mosque of Mecca. In times of sickness or danger the ritual may be relaxed, but not otherwise. Additional or 'supererogatory' prayers are frequently recommended, especially during the night.

The Koran also mentions the noon prayer on Friday, the principal congregational prayer of the week, and enjoins the suspension of work during it. In the same connexion mention is made of the call to prayer (*adhān*). This replaced the use of bells or clappers, which Mohammed abhorred; and the first muezzin (*mu'adhdhin*, reciter of the *adhān*) was his Abyssinian slave Bilāl. Minarets were as yet unknown, and were first adopted, as it would seem, in Syria during the Caliphate of the Umayyads.

Ablution before prayers is strictly enjoined, and the ritual is defined in Sūra v, v. 9: 'When ye rise up to prayer, wash your faces and your hands [and arms] to the elbows, and wipe your heads and your feet to the ankles.' This is the 'lesser ablution' (*wudhū*). The 'greater ablution' (*ghusl*) is a complete washing of the body after major pollutions. If no water is at hand, hands and face may be wiped with fine clean sand. While personal cleanliness is formally demanded of worshippers, the Koran clearly indicates the symbolic meaning which underlies the practice of ablution.[1]

(vi) *Alms*. With the observance of prayer the Koran regularly enjoins the giving of alms (*zakāh*), as the outward sign of piety and means of salvation. In the earlier years the recommendation of alms-giving seems to have referred rather to free-will offerings (*sadaqāt*); but a late passage (lviii, vv. 13–14) clearly distinguishes *sadaqāt* from

---

[1] It is a curious fact that circumcision, though generally regarded as obligatory upon Muslims, is not mentioned in the Koran.

zakāh. This would imply that the latter was already established as an obligatory contribution, presumably at the rate (prescribed in the later law-books) of one-fortieth of the annual revenue in money or kind. It is to be exacted from all who, whether voluntarily or under constraint, enter into the brotherhood of Islam; but it is not a tax. Rather is it to be regarded as a loan made to God, which He will repay many-fold. Free-will offerings are also a means of expiating offences, and are to be given to relations, orphans, the needy, and travellers (ii, v. 211). The objects upon which the revenue from *zakāh* is to be spent are defined (in Sūra, ix, v. 60, though the term used here is *sadaqāt*) as: the poor, the needy, those employed in its collection, those who are to be conciliated, slaves and prisoners, debtors, wayfarers, and the 'Way of God' (see section ix below).

(vii) *Fasting* was prescribed at Medina 'as it was prescribed for those who were before you' (ii, vv. 179–183). It is laid down that the month of Ramadān, the ninth month of the lunar year, is to be observed as a period of fasting, with complete abstinence from food and drink during the hours of daylight. Those sick or on a journey at this time are exempted, but must make compensation by fasting an equal number of days later. In addition, fasting is included amongst the expiations for various offences.

(viii) *Pilgrimage (Hajj)* to the Sacred Mosque at Mecca was also definitely regulated at Medina. The traditional days in Dhu'l-Hijja (the twelfth month) and the traditional ceremonies of going in circuit round the Kaaba, running between the two small eminences of Safa and Marwa in the vicinity, assembling on the ninth day of the month at the hill of Arafāt (some twelve miles east of Mecca), offering sacrifices of sheep and camels at Minā on the way back to Mecca—all these were retained and prescribed in the Koran. Other traditional usages, including the kissing of the Black Stone set in one of the corners of the Kaaba, and the stoning of the pillars representing the Devil in the vicinity of Minā, though not mentioned explicitly, were observed by Mohammed in his pilgrimages, and so were incorporated into the Muslim rite.

As before praying the worshipper must be ritually clean, so also before making the Pilgrimage the worshipper must be in a state of ritual consecration (*ihrām*). This involves firstly the shaving of the head and the discarding of ordinary clothing before entering the territory of Mecca, putting on instead two plain unsewn sheets, so as to leave the head and face uncovered. Thereafter the pilgrim may not hunt, cut his hair or nails, use perfume, cover his head (except in the case of women), or have sexual relations, until after the sacrifice at Minā, when he resumes his normal condition of life.

Although the Pilgrimage constitutes a religious obligation on every Muslim, the obligation is explicitly limited by possession of the necessary means and the physical possibility of getting to Mecca. With this exception, the duties summed up in the four preceding paragraphs constitute the four universally obligatory 'acts of devotion', and together with the *shahāda* or profession of faith form the five 'Pillars of the Faith'.

(ix) *Jihād in the Way of God*. In addition to these obligations, however, the Koran further enjoins Believers in many passages to 'strive in the Way of God'. The duty is formulated in general terms in Sūra ii, vv. 186 sqq., between the regulations for the Fast and the Pilgrimage.

Fight in the Way of God against those who fight against you, but do not commit aggression . . . Slay them wheresoever ye find them, and expel them from whence they have expelled you, for sedition is more grievous than slaying . . . Fight against them until sedition is no more and allegiance is rendered to God alone; but if they make an end, then no aggression save against the evildoers.

While the context suggests that these verses refer primarily to Mohammed's Meccan opponents, two later passages draw a distinction between warfare against the pagans on the one hand and against Jews and Christians on the other.

When the Sacred Months[1] are over, kill those who ascribe partners to God wheresoever ye find them; seize them, encompass them, and ambush them; then if they repent and observe prayer and pay the alms, let them go their way (ix, v. 5).

Fight against those who believe not in God nor in the Last Day, who

---

[1] The Sacred Months were the seventh, eleventh, twelfth, and first months of the Arabian year, when by immemorial custom no raiding or fighting was done.

prohibit not what God and His Apostle have prohibited, and who refuse
allegiance to the True Faith from among those who have received the
Book, until they humbly pay tribute out of hand (ix, v. 29).

As for those who are slain on the Way of God, they are not dead
but 'living in the presence of their Lord, their needs supplied,
rejoicing in the bounty which God hath given them' (iii, vv. 163–4).

(x) Besides these major issues of doctrine, ritual, and obligation,
the Koran contains also a large body of religious and ethical teachings and of legal injunctions. Wine, swine's flesh, gambling, and
usury, for example, are forbidden, along with a number of super-
stitious usages of the pagan Arabs and the making of images or
representations. Dowries, divorce, the guardianship of orphans, and
inheritance are regulated in detail. Penalties are laid down for
certain crimes, such as stealing, homicide, and murder, as well as
for a few minor offences. Slavery is accepted as an institution, but
certain limitations are placed on the rights of owners over slaves
and their good treatment is enjoined. Fraud, perjury, and slander
are repeatedly and severely condemned, and rules of social behaviour
are laid down in several passages. All these and other regulations
served as the foundation upon which the structure of the *Shari'a*, the
Islamic Law, was erected by later generations, as will be explained
in Chapter 6.

In the light of this summary of Koranic religion, some conclusions
may be reached on the relation of Islam to Judaism and Christianity
and the disputed question of its originality. If by originality is meant
an entirely new system of ideas about God and humanity, the relation
between them, and the spiritual significance of the universe, then
Mohammed's intuition was in no way original. But originality in
such a sense has neither place nor value in monotheistic religion.
All religion has developed by a gradual process of revaluation of
existing ideas, as religious thinkers and seers in later generations
have reinterpreted elements present in the thought of earlier generations, giving them fuller significance or setting them in a fresh
relation to the common structure of religious thinking and experience.

So far from professing to bring a new revelation Mohammed

insisted that the Scripture given to him was but a restatement of the faith delivered to the Prophets before him, confirming their Scriptures and itself confirmed by them. Yet the originality of Islam is none the less real, in that it represents a further step in the logical (if not philosophical) evolution of monotheistic religion. Its monotheism, like that of the Hebrew Prophets, is absolute and unconditioned, but with this it combines the universalism of Christianity. On the one hand, it rejects the nationalist taint from which Judaism as a religion did not succeed in freeing itself; for Islam never identified itself with the Arabs, although at times Arabs have identified themselves with it. On the other hand, it is distinguished from Christianity, not so much (in spite of all outward appearances) by its repudiation of the trinitarian concept of the Unity of God, as by its rejection of the soteriology of Christian doctrine and the relics of the old nature cults which survived in the rites and practices of the Christian Church. Here it was helped by its Arabian background, for the desert-man had always scorned the fertility cults of the husbandmen. Their own astral cults were too vague and unorganized to form an effective obstacle to the penetration of monotheistic ideas, and the transition was eased for them by the retention of the characteristic religious ceremony of the nomads, the pilgrimage procession around the common sanctuary and the sacrificial feast in its vicinity. Apart from this one concession to traditional ritual, therefore, Islam set the terms of a new experiment in human religion, an experiment in pure monotheism, unsupported by any of the symbolism or other forms of appeal to the emotions of the common man, which had remained embedded in the earlier monotheistic religions.

In thus setting man as it were face to face with God, without any mediating spiritual or personal elements, Islam necessarily emphasized the contrast between them. In spite of the passages of mystical intuition in the Koran, the dogmatic derived from it could not but start from the postulate of the opposition between God and man, and (as a necessary corollary) the equality of all men in their creaturely relation to God. In this stark contrast lies the original tension of Islam. And however the concrete and literalist minds of the desert-men may have conceived the power and majesty of God, the pleasures of Paradise, and the terrors of Hell, the effect of this tension in rousing religious minds to a sense of responsibility is proved by the explosive and creative force which it manifested century after century.

But the very existence and originality of such a tension set the leaders of the Muslim Church a peculiarly difficult task in meeting the two problems for which all religious systems must find an answer. One is the problem of its appeal to the reasoning mind, which calls for the elaboration of its doctrines in terms acceptable to philosophical thought—or, if this should prove too hard, at least to rational thought. The other is its appeal to the hearts and wills of ordinary men and women. It remained to be seen how far and how long a religion which aspired to be universal could keep the mass of its followers on so stern and exacting a plane of religious obligation and experience.

5

The Tradition of the Prophet

THE COMPILATION of the Koran and the issue of an official text
were essential steps in the development of Islam. They would have
been taken sooner or later, but it is a striking fact that they were
taken so quickly and so resolutely. The speed and vigour of this
action were due partly to the practical demonstration of its urgency.
But they were also in keeping with an attitude of mind which
directed the outlook, and consequently the activity, of the earliest
generation of Muslims, an attitude which we may call traditionalist.
The traditionalist as a Believer accepts Islam as a simple practical
religion, and, if a scholar, makes it his function to assemble all that
can be got together about the teaching and the conduct of the
Prophet. His ideal is to model his own conduct upon the Prophet's
example, without entering into discussion of ultimate whys and
wherefores.

In this spirit the early Medinian community and its disciples
accepted the teaching of the Koran and the heritage of Mohammed,
with a fervour undimmed by philosophical speculation. The realistic
Koranic presentation of God and of man's relation to Him, with the
ritual and ethical precepts inculcated by the Prophet, sufficed (and
suffice to this day) for the faith and practice of the great body of
humble and sincere Believers. But amongst the intellectual leaders of
Islam it represented a primitive stage of simple piety, which passed
in succeeding centuries into a stage of systematization, when elaborate theologies were worked out with the aid of logical methods and
concepts.

The characteristic religious activity, then, of the first century was the collection and transmission of details about the life and actions of Mohammed, and especially those relating to his revelations and the growth of the Muslim community. In view of the profound impress which the personality of the Prophet had left on his adherents, this activity was a spontaneous growth, owing nothing to outside influences. The natural centre of these studies was Medina, where most of the Companions continued to live and where first-hand information was most securely to be found.

Already in pre-Islamic times tradition had played a most important part in Arabian social life. Every tribe prided itself on the 'custom' (*sunna* = *mos*) of its ancestors, and on its adherence to that 'custom'. The Koran speaks of the unchanging *sunna* of Allah and reproaches the Meccans for clinging to the *sunna* of their fathers. The Muslim community also developed its own *sunna*, its proper system of social and legal usages, whether these were taken over from older custom or were set by the Prophet; but in the strict sense the term was applied to those usages only which were not laid down in the Koran. *Sunna*, in the Islamic sense, thus designated the 'custom of the Community' handed down by oral transmission, in distinction from the *kitāb*, the written 'Book'.

After the conquests the *sunna* began to develop in diverging directions in each of the new Arab settlements. Against this, the students of tradition maintained that the term could be properly used only of the usage set by Mohammed himself, either in the form of definite prescription or prohibition or by example. Their view ultimately prevailed, although a relic of the older meaning survived in the name of *Sunnis* or *ahl al-sunna*, 'the followers of the Sunna', applied to the general body of 'orthodox' Muslims who adhered to the 'usage of the Community'. Their opponents, the *Shī'a*, the 'partisans' of Ali, gave the same allegiance to the Sunna of the Prophet, but held the subsequent conduct of the Community to have been illegal. The opposite of *sunna*, namely *bid'a* or 'innovation', also implies rather divergence from the established usage of the Community than from the usage of the Prophet, although, no doubt, for most Sunnis the two were identical.

The *sunna* of the Prophet was handed down in the form of short narratives told by one of the Companions. For example:

Uqba ibn Āmir said 'Someone sent the Prophet a silk gown and he wore it during the prayers, but on withdrawing he pulled it off violently with a gesture of disgust and said "This is unfitting for Godfearing men." '

Such a narrative is called a *hadīth* or 'statement'. Hadīth is thus the vehicle of the *sunna*, and the whole corpus of the *sunna* recorded and transmitted in the form of hadīths is itself generally called 'the hadīth'.

In the earlier historical traditions about Mohammed no special care was taken in their transmission, the substance being more important than the precise form of words. Oral transmission was indispensable in view of the primitive state of the Arabic script, although individuals may have made written notes of hadīths for their own use. Within two or three generations, however, large numbers of hadīths came into circulation, professing to relate statements made by the Prophet on points of law and doctrine. Religious and political parties showed a suspicious readiness to produce sayings of the Prophet in defence of their particular tenets, and as time went on these became more and more categorical and detailed.

It was, in fact, obvious that the Tradition was being invaded by forgeries on a vast scale, sometimes by editing and supplementing genuine old traditions, more often by simple inventions. Partisans winked at the abuse, and even the pious were not averse to giving credence to sayings which emphasized moral or doctrinal points. Students journeyed far and wide 'in pursuit of knowledge', as it was called, and the supply increased with the demand. Legal maxims, Jewish and Christian materials, even aphorisms from Greek philosophy, were put into the mouth of the Prophet and there seemed no limits to the process of fabrication.

For the serious students of the hadīth it therefore became a matter of urgency to establish some method of control by which genuine traditions could be sifted out of the mass of forgeries. The first step was to require the narrator of a hadīth to state his source, and if that person was not himself an original Companion, the source from which he had received it. Each hadīth was thus prefaced by a chain of authorities (*sanad*) going back to the original narrator, and the process was called *isnād* or 'backing'. The tradition quoted above, for example, appears in the standard collection of al-Bukhārī with this *isnād*: 'It was told us by Abdallah ibn Yūsuf who said, it was told us by al-Laith, who had it from Yazīd, who had it from Abu'l-Khair, who had it from Uqba ibn Āmir—he said . . .'

On this basis a science of hadīth-criticism was gradually built up in the course of the second and third centuries. The leading part in its earlier development was apparently taken by the students of law, owing to the need of establishing a solid foundation for the formulation of the Sacred Law, as will be seen later. But the theological and legal study of the Tradition went at first hand in hand, although they ultimately diverged to a certain extent.

The first requirement of the new science was adequate biographical data about the narrators, with special attention to their doctrinal views and their relations as contemporaries. This gave rise to a voluminous literature on the Companions and later generations of scholars, in the form of biographical dictionaries, usually arranged in 'classes', i.e. Muslims of the first generation (Companions), of the second generation (Followers-on), of the third generation (Followers of the Followers), &c. The earliest authoritative work of this kind is the 'Great Book of Classes' of Ibn Saʻd (d. 844) in eight volumes; and in almost every century down to the present time similar biographical dictionaries were compiled, not only of traditionists, but also of legists, of Koran-reciters, and scholars of almost every kind.

The specific application of this biographical material to the purposes of hadīth-criticism was the object of a special branch of study called the 'science of impugnment and justification'. This investigated the bona fides of the guarantors of tradition, their moral character, truthfulness, and powers of memory. A certain subjective element inevitably entered into the matter, so that the judgements of different authorities are often discrepant, and relatively few transmitters of tradition emerge from the ordeal with a completely clean sheet. The method of transmission from narrator to narrator was also studied, under the control of the biographical material. In the *isnād* quoted above, for example, it will be noticed that only the two latest transmitters claim direct personal transmission, whereas the three earlier only 'had it from' or 'on the authority of' one another, implying a possible interval.

Finally, on the results of all these investigations, each hadīth was classified under one of three main categories: sound (*sahīh*), good (*hasan*), or weak (*da'īf*). A 'sound' tradition is one whose *sanad* is carried back without interruption to a Companion by a chain of narrators each of whom is trustworthy; a 'good' tradition is one whose *sanad*, though complete, has one weak link, but which is confirmed by another version. Within each class there are further subdivisions, and indeed the criteria for 'good' traditions vary rather considerably; but the refinements of classification may be omitted here. Most of them are the work of later generations of students, when the science of hadīth-criticism had lost all practical value and developed into a pedantic hair-splitting exercise.

The first written collections of traditions were actually made for legal purposes, not for the sake of hadīth-study. In the early years of the third Islamic century, hadīth-study liberated itself to some extent from the needs of the juristic schools and developed as an independent scholastic discipline. But the results of these investigations were immediately applied afresh to law. The outcome of this renewed convergence of law and tradition was the issue half-way through the same century of the first two critical collections, each claiming the title of *al-Sahīh*. Their authors were respectively al-Bukhārī (d. 870) and Muslim (d. 875). These two works rapidly acquired almost canonical authority, and that of al-Bukhārī in particular (though the less critical of the two) has ever since enjoyed a veneration second only to the Koran.

In view of the place which Bukhārī's *Sahīh* occupies in Muslim religious literature, it is worth while to describe it in fuller detail. The work is divided into 97 'books', sub-divided into 3,450 chapters. Each book is devoted to some large general subject of faith or works, such as prayer, fasting, alms, testimony, buying and selling, surety, marriage. Each chapter, called *bāb* or 'door', contains from one to five or six traditions, together with a heading or rubric indicating the subject or bearing of the contents, and often supplemented by

Koranic texts or other fragmentary traditions. Occasionally a *bāb* is found without any hadīth inserted, or with hadīths but no rubric.

Bukhārī's object, in fact, was to furnish the canon lawyers and theologians with the most carefully scrutinized and authenticated traditions on all matters of faith and conduct, arranged for ready reference. The total number of hadīths quoted is about 7,300, but since many are repeated more than once in different contexts they come down to 2,762 in all. Later Muslim tradition asserted that these were selected by Bukhārī out of some 200,000 hadīths, not counting other tens or hundreds of thousands which he rejected without examination—a very revealing comment (even granting some exaggeration) on the enormous circulation of forged traditions.

Viewed as a whole, the *Sahīh* is a work of immense interest and scrupulous scholarship. Variants are carefully noted, doubtful or difficult points in the *sanads* or texts are glossed. On any careful student the book produces a remarkable impression of honesty combined with piety. It may be true, as has been suggested, that the popular appreciation of Bukhārī's collection was due largely to the fact that he brought together the traditions already accepted in religious circles as a result of the long preceding process of critical examination, but this does not exclude the element of personal worthiness which set, as it were, the seal of authentication upon them.

Several sections of the *Sahīh* have been translated into English, but the only complete version in a European language is one made by MM. Houdas and Marçais into French. It may be of interest, therefore, to summarize here the contents of the first book, which consists of a single *bāb*, although it is not fully typical of the rest. The rubric runs: 'How the beginning of inspiration came to the Apostle of God, and God's saying (Exalted be His Name) "Verily We have inspired thee as We inspired Noah and the Prophets after him."' But immediately after this and before inserting any traditions relevant to the rubric, there is inserted the celebrated tradition, carried back by a direct chain of authorities to the second Caliph, Omar:

I heard the Apostle of God say, By their intentions shall men's works be judged, and to each man shall be only that which he purposed. Whoso hath migrated [i.e. left his tribe to join the Community at Medina] for worldly goods, to attain them, or for a woman, to marry her, his migration (shall be reckoned) only for the purpose for which he migrated.

It would seem that the object of this parenthesis was to warn students of the hadīth against the outward and mechanical application of the letter of the traditions without regard to their spirit. Then follow five traditions; three shorter ones from Mohammed's wife Ā'isha and his cousin Ibn Abbās describing the experience and outward appearance of the Prophet during the reception and recital of the revelations; a lengthy tradition ascribed to Ā'isha in which Mohammed relates the beginning of his mission with the vision of Gabriel and the first words of the revelation; and a still lengthier tradition from Ibn Abbās which is a typical fragment of early Muslim legend recounting an interview between the Roman Emperor Heraclius and the chiefs of the pagan Meccans on the subject of Mohammed.

It must not be imagined that the collections of Bukhārī and Muslim ended the compilation of the hadīth—rather the opposite. The elaboration of the legal systems still required authorities for many matters not dealt with either in the Koran or in the two Sahīhs, and later compilers undertook the necessary task of compiling them, even if, in order to do so, they had to relax the strict rules of criticism to some extent and to include many hadīths which were admittedly less well authenticated or even (though exceptionally) weak. Four works of the next generation were eventually accepted as canonical authorities for this purpose; these were the 'four sunan' of Abu Dāwud (d. 888), al-Nasā'i (d. 915), al-Tirmidhi (d. 892), and Ibn Māja (d. 896), which with the two Sahīhs made up the 'Six Books'. For several centuries more, collections of traditions continued to be made for many purposes and on many different plans. Several of these works also were esteemed by scholars, though they ranked below the collections already mentioned.

To Western scholars the technique of hadīth-criticism by examination of the chain of authorities seems to present some grave defects. A frequent criticism is that it was as easy for forgers to invent an isnād as to tamper with or fabricate a text. But this overlooks the difficulty that the forger would have in getting the isnād (with his name at the end of it) accepted and passed on by scholars of honesty and repute. And that the Muslim critics of tradition were generally honest and pious men must be allowed, even if some Muslims have themselves asserted the contrary. A more fundamental criticism is that the *isnād* technique was elaborated only in the course of the second century. If one looks, for example, at the recorded teachings of al-Hasan of Basra, the exemplar of Muslim piety at the end of the first century, it will be seen that he recites hadīths without any attempt to back up their authenticity with *isnāds*. Ample evidence has been produced to show that the technique itself arose out of the conflict between the traditionists and the older schools of law in Medīna and Iraq which followed the *sunna* of their own communities, and that in the course of this conflict many accepted legal decisions and traditions recently put into circulation, or deriving from later authorities, were provided with formal *isnāds* back to the Prophet, more or less artificially. The historians in their turn adopted the same method of 'improving' the *isnāds* of their materials relating to the life and activities of the Prophet, although there was little need, in their very different case, to supplement the existing traditions by new inventions.

Faced with these facts, some European critics have argued for a more or less radical rejection of the whole system as an artificial creation of later Muslim scholasticism. But this is to go too far. It assumes that Muslim hadīth-criticism was based exclusively upon the formal *isnād*-criteria. This was certainly not the case. There is a curious analogy between the growth of the *hadīth* and that of the early Christian documents, which may be called (in Islamic terminology) Christian hadīth. But the comparison between them also brings out the important differences. Whereas, in a civilization with a tradition of written literature, the earlier and later Christian writings were issued in the real or assumed names of their authors, in the oral literature of the Arabs—confined to poetry, Koran (for the Koran was still orally taught), and hadīth—the only method of transmitting the later developments and expansions of the primitive doctrine was to attach them to the hadīth.

Of all this the Muslim scholars were fully aware. In characteristic fashion this recognition is itself ascribed to the Prophet by several hadīths, such as: 'Whatsoever is said of good speech, that have I said', or 'After my departure the sayings attributed to me will multiply . . . Whatsoever is told to you as my words, compare it with the Book of God; what is in agreement with it is from me, whether I have actually said it or not.' On the other hand, many theologians were deeply disturbed at the way things were going in the invention and distortion of hadīths. But even they found no way of giving currency to their protest except by putting it too into the form of a tradition: 'Whosoever shall repeat of me that which I have not said, his resting place shall be in hell'—a hadīth which found its way in due course into all the canonical collections.

Here, as often in Muslim scholarship, there is a certain unexpressed dislocation between the formal outward process and the inner realities. The *isnād*-criticism has undoubtedly an element of artificiality in it, which conceals (or rather rationalizes) a long process of criticism of the texts themselves, and even Bukhārī admits into his *Sahīh* a number of traditions which do not fulfil his formal conditions of genuineness. The real justification of the system is twofold. In the first place, it gave formal approval to the results achieved by the scholars of the second century in asserting what was felt to be the genuinely Islamic standpoint against deviating tendencies in law and doctrine, and anchored them securely by the device of ascribing them to Mohammed himself. In the second place, it provided a reasonable gaurantee for the future against the infiltration of suspect hadīths. If their contents were purely ethical or homiletic, the *muhaddithūn* or experts in this new branch of learning were inclined to be lenient; but the canons of criticism were more strictly applied to hadīths concerning theological, legal, or ritual matters. On these subjects the theologians were justly suspicious, and the later orthodox jurists had, as we have seen (p. 55), to find the materials they required as best they could.

It is true, on the other hand, that the scholars of the third century, finding a formally perfect hadīth which was generally accepted in scholastic circles as genuine, could only with difficulty reject it or question its bona fides; and that for that reason many hadīths which are clearly suspect on other grounds (like the story of Heraclius and the Meccans) are included in the *Sahīh* works and in other works of religious learning, such as Tabari's Commentary on the Koran. But while the early canonical collections already contain a certain substratum of pious legend and much of the newer ethical and homiletic material which had grown up in the Islamic community as a result of its expansion and contact with older civilizations in Western Asia, the great mass of sectarian traditions of the first and second centuries are only to be found in collections of less authority and repute. The judgements and criteria of the early traditionists, whatever may be regarded as defects in their method, seem at least to have effectively excluded most of the propagandist traditions of the first century and all those of the second, such as those which supported the doctrines of the Shī'a or the claims of the Abbāsids, or which foretold the coming of the Mahdī.

But so far as the later scholars and collections are concerned, it is one of the paradoxes in the history of Islamic science that precisely as the discipline of hadīth-criticism became more and more meticulous, the general body of Muslim theologians and writers became less and less critical. In the later centuries the most patent inventions were cited and accepted without any apparent hesitation and this in turn reflected unfavourably on the scholastic study itself, so that ultimately, in the later collections, the whole isnād-apparatus was discarded altogether or reduced to the name of the first 'authority' and an indication whether the tradition was 'sound', 'good', or 'weak'.

The place occupied by the tradition in the building up of Islamic law and theology will be shown in the following chapters. But before closing this discussion of its development, there is one other aspect of the process which it is of interest to note. Just as, in dealing with the documents of Christian tradition, the task of critical scholarship is directed not only towards isolating the primitive elements in the tradition, but also to tracing the development of thought and practice in the Christian community in successive generations, so too the study of the hadīth is not confined to determining how far it represents the authentic teaching and practice of Mohammed and the primitive Medinian community. It serves also as a mirror in which the growth and development of Islam as a way of life and of the larger Islamic community are most truly reflected. From this historical angle, it is precisely the non-authentic and invented elements in much early and all later tradition that give it special documentary value.

Thus it is possible to trace in hadīths the struggle between the supporters of the Umayyads and the Medinian opposition, the growth of Shi'ism and the divisions between its sects, the efforts of the Abbasids to establish their right to the Caliphate by inheritance, the rise of theological controversies, and the beginnings of the mystical doctrines of the Sūfis. Already in the great collection, containing nearly 30,000 hadīths, of the orthodox doctor Ahmad ibn Hanbal (d. 855) much of this is incorporated. But in later days the different movements within Islam tended to form their own separate collections of traditions. More particularly the Shi'ites, in the next century, composed their own standard works, repudiating the traditions of the Sunnis and proclaiming the validity only of the hadīths derived from Ali and his supporters.

6
The Sharī'a

It is characteristic of the practical bent of the Islamic community
and of its thought that its earliest activity and most highly developed
expression is in law rather than in theology. Several explanations
might be advanced for this fact. It might be said, for example, that
the practical needs of the community-in-being made it necessary to
stabilize and standardize the processes of law long before its intellectual curiosity progressed to the point of asking and answering
metaphysical questions. Or some might argue that the familiarity
with Roman law acquired by the Arabs not only in Syria and Egypt
but also among the Christians in Iraq predisposed them to construct
their own legal system at a much earlier date than Christian controversy and Greek philosophy began to influence Islamic religious
thought. In support of this view it could be pointed out that the first
Muslim schools of law, in the strict sense, arose in Syria and Iraq
before the end of the Umayyad Caliphate in 750. Or again, on more
sociological grounds, it might be suggested that oriental societies, in
contrast to most western societies, have generally devoted much more
sustained and successful efforts to building up stable social organizations, with law as one of their pillars, than to constructing ideal
systems of philosophical thought.

It is possible that the study of law in Islam and the organization
of its elements into some coherent system was influenced or hastened
on by these or other factors. But the impulse itself came from none
of these things. So far as our evidence goes, it seems to show that
in the Umayyad period disputes among the Arab tribesmen were

either settled by tribal customary law administered by their shaikhs or dealt with by the Caliph or his representatives in accordance with their own judgement—both, no doubt, influenced in greater or less degree by the legislation of the Koran. As for Roman law, though some of its formulae and contents percolated into Islamic law, the principles upon which the latter was constructed and (one may even say) the whole spirit of its application were entirely unrelated to those of the Roman jurists. Indeed, from the very beginning, the methods and formulations of Islamic law present a curious combination of positive injunction and theoretical discussion which betrays the atmosphere of the school rather than of the market-place.

Law in the eyes of the Muslim scholars was not in fact an independent or empirical study. It was the practical aspect of the religious and social doctrine preached by Mohammed. For the early Muslims there was little or no distinction between 'legal' and 'religious'. In the Koran the two aspects are found side by side, or rather interwoven one with the other, and so likewise in the Hadīth. The study and interpretation of the Koran involved sometimes the one and sometimes the other, and nearly a century elapsed before scholars began to specialize in one or the other aspect. Ultimately they were distinguished by relative terms: *'ilm*, 'positive knowledge', denoting theology (though not excluding law), and *fiqh*, 'understanding', denoting law (as based on theology). Only at a much later date was the Greek word 'canon' (*qānūn*) adopted to denote administrative rule as distinct from revealed law. (Thus 'canon law' in Arabic should mean the exact opposite of canon law in European usage.)

The connexion between law and religion thus established by Mohammed and adopted by his followers persisted throughout all later centuries. Characteristically, all expositions of Muslim law begin with the 'religious duties' or 'acts of worship', such as ablution, prayer, and pilgrimage. As in other Semitic religions, law is thought of, not as a product of human intelligence and adaptation to changing social needs and ideals, but of divine inspiration and hence immutable. For Muslims its proof-texts were to be found in the Koran and Prophetic Tradition; and on this assumption the jurists and theologians of the second century elaborated a structure of law that is, from the point of view of logical perfection, one of the most brilliant essays of human reasoning.

Before examining the product of this activity, it is of some importance to look a little more closely into the methods followed by the jurists in their endeavour to systematize their material, for the insight which it affords into the character of Muslim epistemology and reasoning.

The Koran and the Tradition are not, as it is often said, the basis of Islamic legal speculation, but only its sources. The real foundation is to be sought in the attitude of mind which determined the methods of utilizing these sources. The first question, then, is not 'What is laid down in the Koran and the Hadīth?', but 'Why are the Koran and the Hadīth accepted as sources of law?', and the second is 'How are their prescriptions to be understood and applied?'

To answer the first question by saying that Koran and Hadīth are accepted as infallible sources because they are the foundations and title-deeds of the religion of Islam is to argue in a circle. The ultimate reason is metaphysical and *a priori*. It is a conviction of the imperfection of human reason and its inability to apprehend by its sole powers the real nature of the Good or indeed any reality whatsoever. Absolute good and evil can therefore be known to men only through a divine revelation mediated through Prophets. By Divine Providence there has been a succession of such Prophets ever since, by the creation of Adam (who was the first of them), mankind has existed on this earth. The revelations accorded to these Prophets were all identical in principle, but formed a gradually developing series adapted to the stages of man's development. Each in turn expanded, modified, and abrogated the preceding revelations. The Koran is the final revelation and therefore contains the final and most perfect solutions for all questions of belief and conduct.

So far the Koran. The argument for the infallibility of the Sunna is rather a consequential and logical than a metaphysical argument. The Koran is comparatively short, and even in this small book the greater part has no direct bearing on dogmatic, ritual, legal, political, and social questions. In theory, the general principles by which all these matters should be regulated are to be found in the Koran, but not all of them are set out with equal clearness and detail. It is therefore essential to interpret and elaborate the relevant texts. The natural, and indeed the only possible interpreter whose judgement can be trusted is the Prophet through whom they were revealed. According to the Koran itself this Prophet was possessed not only of the *kitāb*, the writtten 'book', but also of the *hikma*, the 'wisdom' whereby ultimate principles can be applied to the details and episodes of ordinary life. Consequently, his actions and sayings, transmitted by chains of reliable narrators, form a kind of commentary and supplement to the Koran. From this it was only a step to the further position that this commentary was itself inspired, in that in all his sayings and doings the Prophet was acting under 'tacit inspiration' and thus supplied solutions to the problems of good and evil as final as those of the Koran.

The Koran and Tradition having thus been accepted as infallible sources, how are their rules and indications to be applied? Neither offered a systematic body of legal provisions, but only supplied the materials out of which a system could be constructed. The actual construction of this system thus involved the creation of a new and elaborate science of interpretation or 'roots of jurisprudence'.

Obviously, the foundation of the system was laid by the clear and unambiguous commands and prohibitions found in the Koran and Tradition. Where these exist the exercise of human reason is excluded. But first of all it is necessary to prove their existence. This question does not, of course, arise in the case of Koranic texts (unless there are variant readings which alter the sense), but does arise in the case of texts in the Hadīth. Hence the creation of that study of the authenticity of hadīth with all its complicated disciplines which was outlined in the preceding chapter. In addition, it is necessary to show that the relevant text has not been 'abrogated', if it should happen to be in conflict with another of equal authority.

The requirements of historical criticism having now been satisfied, it next falls to be considered whether the rule formulated in any given case is limited or not in its application. The general principle which was laid down by the jurists was that unless the text itself expressed or implied some limitation (as, for example, to local historical circumstances or to a particular class of persons), then the rule was not limited in any way but was universally applicable at all times.

Lastly it is necessary to determine what the rule means, that is, to establish the literal sense of the text or rule by means of philology and lexicography. This once established, it was held as a general principle that the words were to be taken in their literal sense as commonly used in Arabic speech—excepting, of course, such expressions as were clearly metaphorical (as, for example, the Koranic injunction to 'hold fast to the rope of God').

Where, however, points of law arose which were not covered by a clear statement in Koran or Tradition, the majority of jurists had recourse to analogy (*qiyās*), i.e. the application to a new problem of the principles underlying an existing decision on some other point which could be regarded as on all fours with the new problem. But even this was rejected by the strictest jurists as involving an element of human judgement and therefore fallible.

On this apparently narrow and literalist basis the theologians and lawyers of the second and third centuries worked out not only the law, but also the rituals and the doctrines, which were to be the special property of the Islamic community in distinction from other religious and social organizations. Yet the narrowness is more apparent in theory than in practice, for (as we have seen and shall see again) a great deal became naturalized in Islam from outside sources through the medium of traditions claiming to emanate from the Prophet and in other ways. But because the principles on which this logical structure was built up were immutable, so also the system itself, once formulated, was held to be immutable, and indeed to be as divinely inspired as the sources from which it was drawn. From that day to this, the *Sharī'a* or *Shar'*, as it is called, the 'Highway' of divine command and guidance, has remained in essentials unchanged.

It may be asked how far this inflexibility and stereotyping were inherent in the system of law and theology as they were originally conceived. One might have expected that the work of the theologians and jurists of the second and third centuries would have been open to review and, if necessary, revision by later generations with equal authority within the same limits. The rigidity was due to the introduction of a principle which made its appearance in the community in the first place, it would seem, to give the sanction of legitimacy to its political structure. This was the principle of 'consensus' (*ijmāʿ*).

It is one of the boasts of Islam that it does not countenance the existence of a clergy, who might claim to intervene between God and man. True as this is, however, Islam, as it became organized into a system, did in fact produce a clerical class, which acquired precisely the same kind of social and religious authority and prestige as the clergy in the Christian communities. This was the class of the *Ulamā*,[1] the 'learned' or the 'doctors', corresponding to the 'scribes' in Judaism. Given the sanctity of Koran and Tradition and the necessity of a class of persons professionally occupied with their interpretation the mergence of the Ulamā was a natural and inevitable development, though the influence of the older religious communities may have assisted the rapid establishment of their social and religious authority.

As their authority became more firmly held and more generally conceded by the public opinion of the community the class of Ulamā claimed (and were generally recognized) to represent the community in all matters relating to faith and law, more particularly against the authority of the State. At an early date—probably some time in the second century—the principle was secured that the 'consensus of the community' (which in practice meant that of the Ulamā) had binding force. *Ijmāʿ* was thus brought into the armoury of the theologians and jurists to fill up all the remaining gaps in their system. As the Tradition was the integration of the Koran, so the consensus of scholars became the integration of the Tradition.

Indeed, on a strict logical analysis, it is obvious that *ijmāʿ* underlies the whole imposing structure and alone gives it final validity. For it is *ijmāʿ* in the first place which guarantees the authenticity of the text of the Koran and of the Traditions. It is *ijmāʿ* which determines how the words of their texts are to be pronounced and what they mean and in what direction they are to be applied. But *ijmāʿ* goes much farther; it is erected into a theory of infallibility, a third channel of revelation. The spiritual prerogatives of the

[1] Properly *ʿulamā*, plural of *ʿālim*, 'one possessed of ʿilm' (i.e. religious knowledge).

Prophet—the Muslim writers speak of them as the 'light of Prophecy'—were inherited (in the Sunni doctrine) not by his successors
in the temporal government of the community, the Caliphs, but by
the community as a whole.

When the Muslim community agrees to a religious practice or rule of
faith, it is, in a certain manner, directed and inspired by God, preserved
from error, and infallibly led towards the Truth . . . by virtue of a
special grace bestowed by God upon the community of Believers.[1]

Ijmāʿ thus intervenes more or less decisively in every branch of
Islamic doctrine, law, and state-craft; it may even set aside or super-
sede the strict logical conclusions regarding the authenticity, meaning and application of a given text; it may give support to a tradition
which strict criticism rejects as of doubtful genuineness; and though
it cannot in theory abrogate a direct text of Koran or Tradition, it
may (in the view of the jurists) indicate that 'the law so prescribed
has fallen into disuse'.

When, therefore, a consensus of opinions had been attained by
the scholars of the second and third centuries on any given point,
the promulgation of new ideas on the exposition of the relevant texts
of the Koran and Hadīth was as good as forbidden. Their decisions
were irrevocable. The right of individual interpretation (*ijtihād*) was
in theory (and very largely in practice also) confined to the points on
which no general agreement had yet been reached. As these were
narrowed down from generation to generation, the scholars of later
centuries were limited to commenting and explaining the treatises
in which those decisions were recorded. The great majority of
Muslim doctors held that the 'gate of *Ijtihād*' was shut once and for
all, and that no scholar, however eminent, could henceforth qualify
as a *mujtahid*, an authoritative interpreter of the law; although some
few later theologians did from time to time claim for themselves the
right of *ijtihād*.

There is a certain analogy between this settlement of doctrine by
'consensus' in Islam and the Councils of the Christian Church, in
spite of the divergences of outer form; and in certain respects the
results were very similar. It was, for example, only after the general

---

[1] Santillana, *Instituzioni di Diritto musulmana*, I, 32.

recognition of *ijmāʿ* as a source of law and doctrine that a definite legal test of 'heresy' was possible and applied. Any attempt to raise the question of the import of a text in such a way as to deny the validity of the solution already given and accepted by consensus became a *bidʿa*, an act of 'innovation' (see p. 50), that is to say, heresy.

The most remarkable feature of this whole development is its logical formalism. Although the presuppositions on which it rests may certainly be derived from the Koran, the later scholars of Medina and Iraq, in their zeal to make the system completely watertight, did not hesitate to push the conclusions derived from these presuppositions to their extreme logical limits. The doctrine that Mohammed was 'implicitly' inspired in *all* his sayings was due simply to the necessity of safeguarding his infallibility as the interpreter of the Koran. If it were held that he was inspired in those sayings which interpret the Koran but not in other sayings which refer to the trivial events of daily life, the difficulty of distinguishing between them would arise; and further, as we have seen, the legists needed an infallible source for precisely all these trivial details. Any possibility of questioning whether in fact this or that solution was inspired had to be avoided at all costs, and so the danger was parried by declaring all his acts and sayings inspired. It must not, of course, be assumed that this was anything but an instinctive, almost unconscious, movement of thought.

The same preoccupation with theoretical completeness underlies the doctrine of *ijmāʿ*. Originally it allowed a measure of development (the Caliphate, for example, rests entirely upon *ijmāʿ*), but its function was afterwards circumscribed to the purpose of setting the seal upon the doctrines elaborated by the jurists and theologians and stamping them as unalterable. From a positive and creative principle it was forced into a negative and repressive use.

The conception of law in Islam is thus authoritarian to the last degree. 'The Law, which is the constitution of the Community, cannot be other than the Will of God, revealed through the Prophet.'[1] This is a Semitic form of the principle that 'the will of the sovereign is law', since God is the sole Head of the Community and therefore

[1] Santillana, *Diritto*, I, 5.

sole Legislator. Consequently, to violate the law, or even to neglect the law, is not simply to infringe a rule of social order—it is an act of religious disobedience, a sin, and involves a religious penalty.

We can now examine briefly the content and character of this divine legislation. Muslim jurists lay it down that 'the fundamental rule of law is liberty'. But since human nature is weak, easily led astray, ungrateful, and covetous, it is necessary both in the interests of the individual and in those of the social organism to set certain limits to human freedom of action. These limits constitute the law; and hence Muslim jurists use the term *hadd*, 'limit', in the sense of 'legal ordinance'.

These limits, ordained by the Wisdom and Lovingkindness of God, are of two kinds, corresponding to the dual nature of man as soul and body. As soul and body complement one another in the human organism, so do the two aspects of law complement one another in the social organism. The limits ordained for the soul of man define his relations to God, i.e. prescribe the principles of religious belief and in particular the acts whereby these are given outward expression, namely, the five 'Pillars of the Faith' (see p. 45). Similarly, the limits set to the bodily activities of man define his relations to his fellow-men. These form the subject-matter of law in the narrow sense, i.e. questions of personal status, family organization (including marriage and divorce), holding and disposal of property, commercial activities, and penal law, although the Western distinctions between civil, penal, private, and other kinds of law are not recognized in the Muslim law-books.

The consequence of this was that Law was never quite separate in conception from Duty, and never became fully self-conscious. As the standard definition put it: 'The science of law is the knowledge of the rights and duties whereby man may fitly conduct his life in this world and prepare himself for the future life.' The Sharī'a was thus never erected into a formal code, but remained, as it has been well said, 'a discussion on the duties of Muslims'. This characteristic determines the nature of the judgement passed upon the various activities of which it takes cognizance, a judgement which goes back to the basic conception of a divine legislation mediating absolute standards of Good and Evil. The majority of actions do not come within the scope of law at all, since the initial principle of liberty assumes that in the absence of revealed information about an action it is morally (and therefore legally) indifferent. Such actions are therefore technically called 'permitted'. The remainder are either good or bad in themselves, but in both cases the law recognizes two categories, an absolute and a permissive. Thus the full scheme comprises five grades or classes:

1. Actions obligatory on Believers.
2. Desirable or recommended (but not obligatory) actions.
3. Indifferent actions.
4. Objectionable, but not forbidden, actions.
5. Prohibited actions.

The ethical or ritual element enters, further, not only into the classification of actions but also into the sanctions of law. These are not, in consequence, consistently worked out, and religious penalties frequently supplement or take the place of social or civil penalties.

Such a 'science of classification' bears on its face the marks of its theoretical and rather bookish elaboration. In origin, it was based upon a body of legal practices of heterogeneous provenance: Arab customary law, the commercial law of Mecca, the agrarian law of Medina, elements of foreign (chiefly Syro-Roman) law taken over after the conquests, supplementing or accommodated to the Koran. But since, in Umayyad times, the actual administration of law was largely in the hands of civil and military officers, the formulation of the Revealed Law was left in the hands of theologians and expositors who had little judicial experience in the outer Arab world. The advent of the Abbasid Caliphs brought this scholastic law for the first time to the test of practice, and it was at the beginning of this period, in the second and third centuries of the Muslim era, that the classification was finally systematized.

As the capital of the Abbasids was in Iraq, it was natural that the legal school which they favoured should be that of Iraq. Its reputed founder was Abū Hanīfa (d. 767); and although Abū Hanīfa himself refused to accept judicial office two of his disciples, Abū Yūsuf and Mohammed al-Shaibānī, held high judicial posts and in their writings organized and developed his teaching. This school, called after him the Hanafi school, arose out of the older Iraqi *sunna* and legal schools, adapted to the later growth of Prophetic Tradition, but retained a considerable element of personal reasoning (*ra'y* = *opinio*).

The Medinian school likewise grew out of the 'practice' of Medina, supported by the findings of prominent Medinian jurists of the past. Its champion was Mālik ibn Anas (d. 795), who collected the traditions upon which he, as a practising judge at Medina, based his decisions into a corpus called *al-Muwatta* ('the Levelled Path'), and after whom the school is called the Māliki school.

Less than a generation later, al-Shāfi'ī (d. in Egypt 820), a disciple of Mālik, laid the foundations of the juristic science described earlier in this chapter. The system to which he gave his name combined strict adherence to the now established Prophetic Tradition (which he distinguished from Medinian tradition) with a modification of Hanafi method in the form of analogical deduction (*qiyās*).

In spite of their formal differences and divergences in detail, all three schools grew into substantial agreement on the more important matters. All of them in practice recognized the same sources: Koran, Sunna, Ijmā', and some form of analogical reasoning; and all recognized each other's systems as equally orthodox. Thus they are not to be distinguished as different 'sects' of Sunni Islam, but merely as distinct schools, or in the Arabic expression 'ways' (*madhāhib*, sing. *madhhab*). Any scholar or ordinary Believer might belong to any one, but in the long run they tended to divide the Islamic world between them. At the present day the Hanafi school predominates in Western Asia (except Arabia), Lower Egypt, and Pakistan; the Shāfi'ī in Indonesia; and the Māliki in North and West Africa and Upper Egypt.

Besides these three there were several other schools. The Syrian school of al-Awzā'i (d. 774) disappeared in favour of Mālikism at a very early date. During the third century, a strong traditionalist reaction against the speculative 'innovations' of the previous schools and the Mu'tazilite dialectic was led by two Baghdad doctors, Ahmad ibn Hanbal (d. 855) and Dā'ud al-Zāhiri (d. 883). The Zāhiri school seems never to have gained a wide following, though it counted some outstanding jurists in later centuries, but the Hanbali school had a strong following in Iraq and Syria until the Ottoman conquest. In the eighteenth century it was revived (under the name of Wahhābi) in Central Arabia, and is now the dominant school in most of Central and Northern Arabia. Although recognized by the other schools as a fourth orthodox *madhhab*, its attitude towards them has been generally less tolerant.

Since the formal legal doctrines and definitions of these schools remained substantially unchanged through all the later centuries, there is little to be gained by tracing down and discussing their formidable output of juristic works. But in view of the very widely held view that Islamic Law (or Koranic Law, as it is often called) has remained in a petrified state ever since the 'gate of *Ijtihād*' was closed in the third century, it is of considerable interest to note some of the later developments.

Since the formulation of the Religious Law was totally independent of the secular authority, there could be no question of interference by Caliphs or Sultans with its rules and decisions. The secular authorities were bound to recognize it and to provide for its due administration by the appointment of judges (*qāḍīs*) in all parts of their territories. But although there is little that can be called legislation by the State until the rise of the Ottoman Empire, yet from an early date the secular authorities intervened to a certain extent in judicial administration by holding courts 'for the redress of wrongs' (*mazālim*). In these a somewhat arbitrarily modified form of the religious law was applied, with or without the collaboration of the official *qāḍīs*.

In the religious courts, and sometimes in *mazālim* courts as well, it was a common procedure to submit a summary of any important case to a qualified jurist for his opinion. Such a consultant was called a *muftī*, and his reply was embodied in a *fatwā* or statement of the legal issues. As a rule the *muftīs* maintained their independence of the secular administration, but in the Ottoman Empire they were graded in the official hierarchy, ranking below the *qāḍīs*, and the Chief Muftī of Constantinople, who was entitled Shaikh al-Islām, was the highest religious authority in the Empire.

The collections of *fatwās* by eminent jurists are thus a much more important source for the study of legal usage and development than the stereotyped textbooks of the *madhāhib*. In them there is reflected the long struggle which went on for centuries (and still continues) between the Religious Law and local customary law in many Islamic countries, and the steady pressure of the religious leaders to assimilate local usages (*'ādāt*) to the standards of Islamic law.

In spite of these derogations from its authority, the Sharī'a always remained in force as an ideal and a final court of appeal, and by its unity and comprehensiveness it formed the main unifying force in Islamic culture. Its very lack of flexibility contributed to this result by preventing divergences and disintegration into purely local systems. It permeated almost every side of social life and every branch of Islamic literature, and it is no exaggeration to see in it, in the words of one of the most penetrating of modern students of the subject, 'the epitome of the true Islamic spirit, the most decisive expression of Islamic thought, the essential kernel of Islam'.[1]

[1] *G. Bergsträsser's Grundzüge des Islamischen Rechts*, edited by Joseph Schacht, p. 1.

7

Orthodoxy and Schism

SIDE BY side with the elaboration of the logical framework of law which has been described in the previous chapter went the elaboration of orthodox theology. This also was the work of many generations. Islam, as we have seen, came out of Arabia as a coherent doctrine, but its theological formulation was still in a fluid state, and it may be that the very extent of territory over which it spread contributed to keep it plastic for a longer time than might otherwise have been required, owing to the varieties of religious thought and experience upon which it acted and which reacted upon it in their turn.

In all the provinces of Western Asia we see Islam at first assuming more or less distinct features, according to the degree of influence which was exerted by the local environment. In the cities of the Hijaz it tended to set in the moulds of the first generations of practical unspeculative piety; in Syria it began to be influenced by Hellenistic Christian thought; in Iraq it became infected with various Gnostic doctrines; amongst the unsettled Arab tribesmen of the borderlands it became an instrument of nomadic cupidity and love of plunder, sublimated into fanaticism; in certain districts of Persia it was adopted as the cloak of a modified dualism. It would have been difficult for a contemporary to prophesy which of all these multifarious forms would emerge as the definitively orthodox or 'official' version of the Islamic faith, more especially as all, with the exception of the fanatical doctrines of the tribesmen, were at first tolerated in greater or less degree, and no man who proclaimed the sole divinity of Allah and the prophetic mission of Mohammed was excluded from the Muslim fold.

The establishment of an orthodox system was thus a gradual process, in which political considerations and political action played a large part (as always in the establishment of orthodox systems), though more often by consolidating than by determining the leading tendencies. The first factor which contributed towards it was the enormous moral preponderance of the Arabs in the Islamic Empire, a moral preponderance which long survived their political preponderance. Here and there voices might be raised against the Arabs, but in the field of religious thought they were ineffective against the weight of *Araberthum*, the Arab idea. The inner history of the Islamic civilization cannot be understood unless that fact is fully realized and given its due place.

Now the centre of this *Araberthum* was Medina, the nucleus whence Islam had spread, and moreover the home of all the earliest religious studies in Islam. It was in Medina that the Koran received its final form, that the Tradition was first collected, and that the earliest application of linguistic and historical studies to the sources of the Muslim religion was made. From the very earliest times students from all countries, whether Muslim-born or converts, Arabs or non-Arabs, flocked to Medina, and received there from the lips of the actual contemporaries of the Prophet, and from those who had lived in the closest intimacy with those contemporaries, the pure doctrine of the new religion. The schools in other countries had a purely local significance; Medina alone was the universal school.

This pre-eminence was strengthened by another factor as well. In the religious theory of Islam, Church and State were one and indivisible; but in fact the delicate moral and religious ties by which the early Caliphs had exercised authority over the Muslim body-politic were roughly snapped in the fourth decade after the Hijra, and in their place was substituted the authority of the military power. Thus Church and State were in practice disjoined; but at Medina the fact was never admitted, and it remained the head-quarters of the religious opposition, denouncing the betrayal of its theocratic ideal and the usurpation of power by worldly rulers. The great bulk of scholastic religious opinion in the Empire shared this feeling, and the stand made by the scholars of Medina raised their prestige, even amongst those who did not fully share their theological conservatism.

By these means, the school of Medina effectively contributed to maintain a general uniformity amongst the lesser local schools of Arab theologians, the most important of which was that in Iraq. Moreover, it stamped upon this nascent universal Chuch its own practical and pietistic ethos, so determining its fundamental characteristics, to which all later developments had ultimately to conform. And perhaps, a matter of scarcely less importance, by thus dissociating the religion of Islam from the political organization, it maintained religion above the sphere of politics and did not involve Islam in the overthrow of Arab political supremacy.

The doctors of Medina reaped their reward when the new Abbasid dynasty established its supremacy and removed the capital of the Empire to Iraq. Orthodoxy, of the Medinian brand, became one of the planks in their platform, and they made it their business to give their moral support at least to the teachings of Medina. Some went farther even than giving merely moral support, by beginning a species of active persecution of the most heretical forms of Islam and more especially the gnostic and dualistic perversions. Gradually the definition of orthodoxy was thus being tightened up. Already the fanatical interpretation of the tribesmen (the extremer Kharijite doctrine) had been rejected as heresy—now the extremer gnostic and dualistic interpretations were equally rejected. Both of these survived, but as definitely heretical sects, and we shall return to them later. There still remained other interpretations and in particular one interpretation, which was infinitely more difficult to isolate and combat. This was the Hellenistic interpretation, maintained by the Mu'tazilite school, and for some two centuries more the struggle between these two conceptions occupied the central place in orthodox Islam.

The points at issue were at bottom metaphysical. Oriental philosophy had never appreciated the fundamental idea of justice in Greek philosophy, and it was this which the representatives of the Hellenistic interpretation were attempting to accommodate within Islam. The stricter schools held to the Oriental conceptions of God as Infinite Power and Infinite Love and Mercy; the Mu'tazilites conceived of God as Infinite Justice. This their opponents regarded as setting limitations upon the Power of God—arbitrary limitations because the requirements of absolute justice were expressed in terms derived from human reason. The argument crystallized out from the philosophical into the theological plane in the problem of Free Will and Predestination, a question on which both sides could point to texts in the Koran to support their case, as was shown in a previous chapter.

In the second place, the Hellenistic school, with its more developed philosophical training, regarded the orthodox doctrine of the Attributes of God (Hearing, Speech, Sight, Willing, etc.) as endangering, if not actually contradicting His Unity. Here again the argument became centred on one point, the Speech of God, and since the Koran is the Speech of God in one sense, it took the (at first sight) strange theological form of affirming on the orthodox side, and denying on the other, that the Koran was uncreated and eternal, with the still more curious result that the opponents of Hellenistic philosophy reaffirmed without realizing it the Hellenistic doctrine of the Logos.

In the majority of modern textbooks, the Mu'tazilites are described as Rationalists or even as Free-thinkers (*Freidenker*). But this is now recognized to be a serious misrepresentation. Until recently, our information about them was derived exclusively from orthodox (i.e. hostile) sources, and they have been regarded in consequence as merely an opposition theological party of no great importance except as the source of these dogmatic conflicts. The recovery of a few Mu'tazilite works is beginning to show them in a new light, as a group of thinkers and teachers who rendered invaluable services to the cause of Islam amongst the peoples of the lands conquered by the Arabs. Between the simple doctrines of Medinian piety and the long tradition of Hellenistic culture and gnosticism in Western Asia there was a gap which it was difficult to bridge over. It was the existence of this gap which was responsible for the great outcrop of strange heresies (especially in Iraq) during the first and second centuries, and it was this gap which was eventually closed by the early Mu'tazilites, who were at once sincere Muslims and able to formulate the Islamic faith in terms which were acceptable to the educated non-Arabs.

The Mu'tazilite movement began, indeed, at the end of the first century as an ethical reaction against the doctrinal and practical excesses of the fanatical Kharijites, on the one hand, and against the ethical laxity of the political conformists (known as the Murji'ites) on the other. Their first doctrinal position is described in consequence, as 'the intermediate position'. While they rejected the Kharijite insistence of 'works' as the sole criterion of faith, they stressed the responsibility of the Believer as against the Murji'ite emphasis on the sufficiency of faith, irrespective of 'works'. This also led them to lay greater stress on those passages of the Koran which assert man's responsibility and power of choice, since it was precisely in the doctrine of predestination that the Murji'ites took refuge. In its beginnings, therefore, the leaders of the Mu'tazila were rigid puritans, rather than rationalists; their teachings were perfectly compatible with (and indeed based upon) the Koran, and we shall probably not be far wrong in regarding them as the most active and vigorous section among the orthodox Sunni teachers in Iraq. It has, indeed, sometimes been a source of embarrassment to later orthodox opponents of the Mu'tazila that both the great saint al-Hasan of Basra and the great jurist Abū Hanifa show more than a hint of what were later called Mu'tazilite leanings in their doctrine.

During the second century we catch little more than glimpses of the Mu'tazilites. But these glimpses are revealing, for they display them to us as the leaders in an intense missionary movement, directed especially against the dualist or Manichaean heresies which were still widespread amongst both the old-established Arab population and the Aramaeans of Iraq. It was partly due, in all probability, to this struggle with the dualists that the Mu'tazilites were brought into contact with Greek logic and philosophy. The great movement of translation of Greek works into Arabic followed, and was especially active at the beginning of the third century, when for twenty-five years Mu'tazilite influence was dominant at the Court. All the Mu'tazilite philosophical schools belong to the third century, and were obviously the outcome of this activity.

This is the aspect of Mu'tazilism with which we are most familiar, and from which it has acquired the appearance of a rationalist movement. Yet the change in its essential character was not as great as it might appear. It was still, in ethics and practice, a puritan school, becoming, indeed, more positive and rigid in its attitude as controversy with the predestinarians increased in violence. For after the fall of the Umayyads the dispute over predestination began to lose its immediate political importance and to take on a more theological character, with the majority leaning towards it and against the Mu'tazilite position.

As for the philosophical schools, it would seem that most or all of them were composed of small groups of disciples of individual theologians, who did not necessarily represent any general body of doctrine. These thinkers developed, by the aid of Greek logic, new theological systems in order to defend their dogmatic positions, and as time went on they advanced more and more boldly into the field of metaphysics. They carried the advanced wing of orthodox scholarship part of the way with them, but the latter stopped short when the Mu'tazilite extremists began to force Muslim doctrines into the mould of Greek concepts and to derive their theology speculatively from Greek metaphysics instead of the Koran.

It could be argued very plausibly that the causes of the successful reaction of the orthodox against the Mu'tazilites had little to do in fact with the external slogans of Predestination and the Uncreated Koran. It was the lengths to which they pushed their three principal doctrines that led to their undoing. The first, called the doctrine of Promise and Threat, governed their practical ethical teaching in regard to individual responsibility. By their dogmatic intolerance and their attempt to use coercion to gain their cause they created a strong current of opposition which was ready to fasten on any pretext to discredit them. And plenty of pretexts were supplied by the philosophical developments of their two other main dogmas, the doctrines of Unity and Justice. In their endeavours to exclude every shadow of anthropomorphism from the concept of God, Mu'tazilite thinkers were forced either into something very like the Christian hypostases or else into a system of abstract negations which left nothing for ordinary Believers to fasten on, and contrasted strongly with the vividly personal figure of Allah presented by the Koran.

Thrown into the wide sea and utter freedom of Greek thought, their ideas had expanded to the bursting-point and, more even than a German metaphysician, they had lost touch of the ground of ordinary life, with its reasonable probabilities, and were swinging loose on a wild hunt after ultimate truth, wielding as their weapons definitions and syllogisms.[1]

More especially by their exaltation of the principle of justice they seemed to erect an *a priori* concept into an absolute even over Allah.

So the breaking-point was reached. In the daily practice of religion they had shown themselves harshly dogmatic, lacking the human charity, tolerance, and broadmindedness of the simple Muslim faith, even to the extent of persecuting their opponents in the day of their power. In their theology they had produced a vacuum and—far worse —had accorded to the products of human reason an absolute value above the Word of God. The orthodox rightly rejected these pretensions, for in religion anthroposophy is a more insidious solvent than anthropomorphism. The right wing of the Mu'tazilites, who in their search for some synthesis of philosophy with orthodox doctrine had been gradually drawing apart from the rationalist left wing, threw in their lot with the defenders of the Sunna. Applying the methods of Greek dialectic to the support of the Koran and the Hadith, they evolved a new orthodox scholasticism and defeated the Mu'tazilites on their own ground.

This victory is associated with the names of al-Ash'ari of Baghdad and al-Māturīdi of Samarqand at the end of the third century of the Muslim era. On the problem of free-will, al-Ash'ari reconciled the predestinarian dogma with the requirements of justice by founding on certain Koranic texts a doctrine of 'acquisition', whereby man 'acquires' the responsibility for his actions although they are willed and created by God. In regard to the Divine Attributes, the scholastics maintained the doctrine of their eternity, but only by applying the Mu'tazilite principle of negation of anthropomorphic concepts. The rigour of the Mu'tazilite ethic was softened by laying more stress on the doctrine of intercession, and its utilitarian aspect countered by the reassertion of the absolute freedom of God to punish or reward as He wills. Finally, while admitting that by

[1] D. B. Macdonald, *Development of Muslim Theology*, p. 140.

Divine 'custom' certain so-called 'effects' normally follow on certain 'causes', they removed the limitations set by the doctrine of natural causation upon the absoluteness of God's power by means of a complex atomic theory which denied any necessary relation between 'cause' and 'effect'.

It was probably to the good of Islam that Mu'tazilite rationalism, having done its work but not known where to stop, was defeated. Had it been successful, it is doubtful whether the popular movements out of which, as will be seen in the next chapter, the regeneration of Islam was to come, could possibly have been tolerated, much less accommodated, within the framework of orthodoxy. Sooner or later the unity of Islamic culture would have suffered violent disruption and Islam itself might have succumbed under the blows of its enemies. But Mu'tazilism did not at once disappear. Its adherents lingered on, still distinguished for strictness in their practice of religious duties, chiefly in Basra and in Eastern Persia, and some of its doctrines found fresh scope in the other great heretical community of the Shi'a.

Meanwhile the orthodox had themselves split into two camps, the scholastics (*mutakallimūn = loquentes*) and the 'people of the Hadīth'. Even in the service of orthodoxy philosophy and logic were suspect; the old school of Medina, in its more moderate Mālikite and Shāfi'ite formulations, and in the extremer and more fanatical wing formed by the disciples of the Baghdad doctor Ahmad ibn Hanbal, still remained hostile to studies tainted by their foreign origin and philosophical associations. In Baghdad itself the scholastics went at times in fear of their lives, until a century and a half later, when, about 1065, the Ash'arite system was established as the main theology of Sunni Islam, largely through the influence (it is thought) of the great Persian vizier Nizām ul-Mulk.

Yet, perhaps, the traditionalists were wiser than they knew, for one result of the importation of Greek dialectic was to concentrate the labours of scholars and theologians upon dogmas and formulas, to the loss of the vital element of personal religion. Had there been nothing else to rekindle the flame, orthodoxy would surely have perished in its own victory. But one by-product of the introduction of scholasticism must not pass unnoticed. It made possible the activities of that remarkable series of medieval Arabic philosophers, al-Kindi (d. 873), al-Fārābi (d. 950), Avicenna (Ibn Sīnā, d. 1037), Avempace (Ibn Bāja, d. 1138), and Averroes (Ibn Rushd, d. 1198) —to mention only a few outstanding names. Though many of them were far from orthodox, their works are among the glories of the Islamic civilization; and there is no need to dwell here upon their services to philosophical thought directly and through the transmission of Greek philosophy to medieval Europe.

In turning to deal with sectarian movements, it must be stressed that by 'sects' are meant those systems of Islamic doctrines and beliefs which are repudiated by the orthodox generally and by one another as heretical. Within the orthodox community itself there have been and still are a number of different 'schools' (Hanafi, Māliki, Shāfi'i, Hanbali) which are all mutually tolerated (see pp. 69–70 above), and in addition to these somewhat legal divisions there have entered into orthodox Islam many later practices and rituals, though not always without opposition. Yet it may be said that as a general rule, the Sunni principle has been to extend the limits of toleration as widely as possible. No great religious community has ever possessed more fully the catholic spirit or been more ready to allow the widest freedom to its members provided only that they accepted, at least outwardly, the minimum obligations of the faith. It would not be to go too far beyond the bounds of strict truth to say, in fact, that no body of religious sectaries has ever been excluded from the orthodox Islamic community but those who desired such an exclusion and as it were excluded themselves.

It is this point precisely which distinguished the earliest sect of Islam, the so-called Khawārij or Khārijites (i.e. 'Seceders'). In their original dogmas they diverged from the Sunni majority on no matter of importance. They broke away merely on a point of practice. It is laid down as the duty of every Muslim to exhort men to do the good and restrain them from doing evil. The orthodox—which is to say, the community as a whole—accepted this obligation with the proviso that due regard must be given to circumstances in putting it into practice. The Khārijites—who were mainly nomads and semi-nomads in Mesopotamia and the fringes of Iraq—rejected the condition, and insisted on it as an absolute duty to be pursued in season and out of season, even at the cost of life itself. In other words they were religious extremists, and their fanaticism led them to the conclusion that those Muslims who temporized on this point were backsliders and apostates, indeed no Muslims at all, and that they themselves were the only true Muslims. Armed with this principle, they made open war on the community, and thus put themselves outside the pale of orthodoxy. The fortunes of the early Khārijites do not concern us here, but eventually their more moderate leaders formulated systems which have survived in small puritanical communities in Southern Algeria, Oman, and Zanzibar. Thus early, Islam rejected the doctrine of religious fanaticism. At a later day, in the eighteenth and early nineteenth century, we shall find the same lesson enforced on the Wahhābi reformers of Arabia.

The case of the other main sect in Islam—the only important schismatic sect, in fact—is different. The Shi'a began as a political movement amongst the Arabs themselves. Ali, the son-in-law of the Prophet and fourth Caliph of Islam, had made his capital at Kūfa in Iraq. When, on his death, the political centre of Islam was shifted to Syria, the opposition of the Arabs of Kūfa to the Arabs of Syria took the form of a legitimist agitation, aiming at the restoration of the house of Ali to the Caliphate. Gradually this political aspiration created for itself a doctrinal basis, opposed to the accepted doctrine of the community, namely, the doctrine of the exclusive right of the house of Ali to the Caliphate. This involved the repudiation of the first three Caliphs, Abū Bakr, Omar, and Othmān, as usurpers, and this denunciation of three of the most revered Companions has always remained the chief offence of Shi'ism in the eyes of orthodox Muslims. But in all other matters of law, as in theology and religious practice, Shi'ism had as yet no distinctive doctrine. This early Shi'ism has left a memorial to this day in Morocco, which is Shi'ite in its political organization, but orthodox Sunni in its theology and law.

At a very early stage, however, the Shi'ite name was used to cover a number of totally different activities, and served as a cloak for the introduction into Islam of all sorts of old oriental beliefs, Babylonian, Persian, and even Indian. The conversion of large numbers of the earlier inhabitants of the conquered countries necessarily led to a widespread unsettlement of religious belief, which favoured the spread of esoteric sects, and led to the religious struggles of the early centuries. The Hellenistic elements as a rule attached themselves to the Sunni or majority party, while the older Asiatic beliefs tended rather to attach themselves to the person of Ali. From their very nature, however, such beliefs were held and propagated mainly by non-Arabs, and more especially by the mixed population of Iraq. There are indications also that Shiʻism in the early centuries was among the people the standard rather of a social revolt against the Sunni ruling classes than of a theological opposition to the Sunni doctrines. It should be said at once that the still far too prevalent view that Persia was the original home of Shiʻism has no foundation at all, and it is noteworthy that converts from Zoroastrianism adopted in general the Sunni rather than the Shiʻite faith.

The principle which was common to practically all these quasi-Shiʻite sects was that parallel to the outward interpretation of the Koran there existed an occult interpretation and a body of secret knowledge. This was *ex hypothesi* transmitted by Mohammed to Ali, and by Ali to his heir. The various sects differed as to who was the heir of Ali, and it is remarkable that hardly any of them attached themselves in this connexion to the line of direct descendants of Mohammed who were the successors of Ali in the view of the legitimist Arab Shiʻism of Kūfa, but rather to the other descendants of Ali. Moreover, while the Arab Shiʻa broke away from the community only on the question of the political headship of Islam, the esoteric sects went much farther in attributing to the Imām—as they styled the head of the Community—a spiritual function which the orthodox theologians always refused to the Caliph. In orthodox Islam the Caliph has no interpretative functions and cannot define dogma; he is simply the political and religious leader of the Community. But for those who held that the occult interpretation of the Koran was known exclusively to the line of Imāms, the only authoritative source of doctrine was the Imām himself. Thus on the one hand their religion was centred on a principle of absolute personal authority, foreign both in politics and religion to the orthodox theory, and on the other hand it permitted a much wider measure of development and adaptation to the circumstances of successive generations under the theoretical guidance of the divinely inspired Imām.

Gradually this doctrine of the Imāmate crystallized into definite theological form. The Imāms acquire a superhuman character, by virtue of the supernatural qualities which they possess. In accordance with the old Babylonian Light-philosophy, this is expressed by the doctrine that in them is incarnated the Divine Light which has descended through successive generations of Prophets from the time of Adam. Some Shi'ite sects even went so far as to regard Ali and the Imāms after him as incarnations of the Godhead itself, but these, though they are still to be found in various parts of the Muslim world, may be disregarded here as exaggerated and unrepresentative views. Similar fragments remain of an opposition doctrine which attributed to the Umayyad Caliphs Yazīd and Marwān much the same divine attributes, especially the Yazīdi sect in Northern Iraq. Of much greater importance is the consequence which was drawn from the original doctrine, namely, that the Imām is sinless and infallible, for this dogma is one of the fundamental doctrines of the greater body of Shi'ites to the present day.

It is not yet clear by what stages these two original forms of shi'ism were welded together, the Arab legitimist Shī'a and the esoteric Shi'ism. But in the third and fourth centuries of the Muslim era the process was already far advanced. The qualities of the gnostic Imāms were transferred to the descendants of the Prophet through Ali and the Prophet's daughter Fātima, and the gnostic doctrines were adopted as the religious constitution of the Shi'a sect. The majority of the minor sects disappeared, leaving the field to three principal groups of Shi'ites.

Of these three, the Zaidis, still dominant in the highlands of Yemen, stand closest to the old legitimist Shi'ism and to orthodox Sunni Islam. They recognize a continuing series of Imāms, to whom no supernatural qualities are ascribed. The majority or Imāmi sect, now the official religion of Persia and with a following in India, Iraq, and Syria, recognizes twelve Imāms; the last of these Mohammed al-Muntazar ('the Expected One'), disappeared about the year 873, and his return is still looked for. The most extreme group, the Ismā'īlis, broke away over the succession to the sixth Imām; they were represented in the Middle Ages by the popular revolutionary movement of the 'Carmathians' (Qarmatis), the Fātimid Caliphate in Egypt (969–1171), and its offshoot, the 'Assassins', whose modern successors still have a following in India and East Africa, under the headship of the Aga Khan.

In the course of time the Imāmi system of doctrine and law has diverged very considerably from that of the Sunnis. The Imāmis do not, of course, accept the principle of *ijmā'*, and in the absence of the Imām, the leading theologians, called Mujtahids (p. 66), exercise an extensive authority in religious and legal matters. In law their chief peculiarity is the permission of temporary marriage, and in religious practice the doctrine of *taqīya* or dissimulation, a relic, probably, of medieval persecution. But in regard to the five 'Pillars of the Faith' they differ only on a few points of detail, minor in themselves although they have acquired an exaggerated importance from a thousand years of embittered controversy. At various times attempts have been made to heal the schism on the basis of recognition of the Imāmi system as a fifth orthodox 'school' by the name of 'Ja'fari' (after the sixth Imām, Ja'far al-Sādiq, whose authority is accepted also by the Sunnis), but these attempts have so far always proved unavailing.

Nevertheless, although its doctrines as a whole were rejected by the orthodox, Shi'ism has exercised a powerful influence in several departments of Sunni thought and practice. The Shi'ite veneration for Ali and his descendants is reflected in the sympathetic attitude of Sunni historical tradition towards them. The doctrine of the Divine Light and the sinlessness of the Imām was taken over and applied, not to Ali himself but to Ali's master, the Prophet Mohammed, and in conjunction with other causes supplied the basis for an enthusiastic veneration of the Prophet, which has ever been one of the strongest spiritual influences in Sunni Islam. The main channel through which these influences, together with other Shi'ite reminiscences, penetrated into the orthodox system was the mystical movement which goes by the name of Sūfism. To this we must now turn.

8
Sūfism

SCHOLARS AND historians are naturally prone to fall into the error (especially erroneous in dealing with the Orient) of assuming that because an order, a dogma, or a regulation is set down in black and white, it thereby acquires practical force as law, theology, or ceremonial. Nothing can be less like the truth. The elaboration of a dogmatic law set a theoretical standard which was gradually and partially approached in certain relations but never fully applied. Similarly, the formulation of an orthodox theology was the work, and excited the interest of only a comparatively small body of scholars; to the great mass of Muslims this dogmatic superstructure was, continued to be, and (one might almost add) still is a matter of general indifference. The cause of this was not altogether either apathy or ignorance. It may have been in part due to the fact that the more developed theological systems were largely negative and substituted for the vivid personal relation between God and man presented by the Koran an abstract and depersonalized discussion of logical concepts. A strong religious sentiment is not likely to be roused—or, if it exists, to be moved to enthusiasm—by the orthodox solution of the problem of the Divine Attributes as it is expressed in the words of one of the standard textbooks of the Islamic faith: 'They are not He nor are they other than He.'

Consequently the elaborate theological system did not in any respect represent the practical religious beliefs of the people, and in fact, the majority of theologians very strongly held the view that it should not even be communicated to the masses. Nor did it even

command the adherence of great numbers of the educated for several
centuries after the Mu'tazilite conflict. The Hellenistic spirit, though
banished from orthodox circles, long continued to influence the
thought of those who were now called heretics, or at least suspected
of being heretics, until political and economic disasters put an end
to all independent intellectual activity. But the influence of the
philosophical school was a diminishing factor in the later development of Islam, and it is rather to popular religion that we must
turn for an understanding of its course.

The movement of popular religion in Islam is closely connected
with the history of Islamic asceticism and mysticism. Professor
Massignon, in a brilliant survey of the whole field of early Islamic
mysticism,[1] has sought to prove that the mystical movement was
the direct heir of primitive Muslim asceticism, itself derived from
the Koran and the practice of the Prophet. But even if this may
be granted, it will be remembered that the groundwork of the
asceticism of the Koran is identical with that of Eastern Christianity,
and, in consequence, in the development of Islam outside Arabia the
two systems cannot always be disentangled. What seems certain, at
least, is that the mystical sense of the Presence of God, which was
implicit in Mohammed's activity as prophet, found no response in
the pragmatic and unintrospective realism of his immediate Arab
followers. But by contrast their religious devotion was, at its best,
the outcome of a profound spiritual experience stimulated by
Mohammed's preaching of the Judgement.

Of all the great religions of Western Asia, Islam has generally
been regarded as the most worldly and least ascetic. Several reasons
may be adduced for this judgement, such as the condemnation of
celibacy, the absence of a priesthood with spiritual functions, and
above all that preliminary compromise with the exigences of political
life which, attained by Christianity only after three centuries of
existence, was reached in Islam during the lifetime of its founder.
Yet amongst the very earliest generations of Muslims, in all parts
of the Islamic world, there were many men who brought the spirit
of devotion into their daily activities, and to whom Islam was a

[1] *Essai sur les Origines du Lexique technique de la Mystique musulmane,*
Paris, 1922.

discipline of the soul and not merely a collection of external rituals. Their creed was a stern ascetic creed, which bade every man go about his work with the fear of eternal punishment ever before his eyes, remembering that this world is but a temporary habitation, and that every gift it has to offer, power, riches, pleasure, learning, the joy of parenthood, is vanity and temptation—not indeed to be rejected or avoided, but to be used with a deep sense of the awful responsibilities which they entail. The highest type of this early asceticism is al-Hasan of Basra (643–728), whose memory remains fragrant in Islam to this day.

In the second century of the Hijra it was from the ranks of the ascetics that there arose those popular preachers in whom the zeal of the old Nestorian missionaries was reborn and who were the real missionaries of Islam amongst the people. The name by which these preachers were known, *qussās*, 'story-tellers', indicates their method. In the form of sermons or commentaries on Koranic texts they stuffed the minds of their hearers with materials derived from the most heterogeneous sources—ancient Arabian legends, Christian, Zoroastrian, and even Buddhist stories, materials from the Gospels and Jewish Haggada, and all the inherited lore of ancient Syria and Babylonia. Amongst this mass of material, two sources, Christianity and Gnosticism, stand out most prominently. But the contributions of both were pressed into an Islamic mould, however repugnant they might be to primitive ideas. Among the most significant of these grafts upon the stem of Islam was the transformation of the Second Advent of Christ into a doctrine of the coming of the Mahdi, the 'rightly-guided one' who will effect the final victory of Islam by means of a divine catastrophe. Another, of equal importance for the future of Islamic religious thought, was the evolution of the doctrine of the person of Mohammed. We have already seen that Shi'ite influences contributed to this evolution; but alongside these there were superimposed upon the natural reverence of the Believer for the person of the Prophet several of the Christian ideas of the person of Jesus.

Many of the miracles and sayings of the Gospels, and of the legends with which the Eastern churches had surrounded the figure of the Founder of their faith, were transferred to Mohammed. In

early Muslim mysticism outside Arabia Jesus still occupies a place
alongside and little if at all inferior to Mohammed, but gradually
the figure of Mohammed transcends the other, until at the end of
the third century we find in the works of the great mystic al-Hallāj
a hymn to the Prophet in which Christian and Gnostic images are
fused into a triumphant synthesis:

All the Lights of the Prophets proceeded from his Light; he was before
all, his name the first in the Book of Fate; he was known before all things
and all being, and will endure after the end of all. By his guidance have
all eyes attained to sight. . . . All knowledge is a drop from his ocean, all
wisdom a handful from his stream, all times an hour from his life.

Here, and not in the abstractions of the theologians, is the true
spirit of popular Islam, and to this Arabia contributed nothing but
the historical existence of Mohammed. Apart altogether from
doctrines and beliefs it is interesting to note how tenacious Christian
usages were, in spite of the change of faith. Well down into the
later Middle Ages, the Christian festivals survived alongside the
official feasts of Islam as the great public festivals of the Mohammedan world.

There is room here only for a brief summary of the beginnings of
the mystical movement in Islam which goes by the name of Sūfism.
The origin of the term Sūfi is complex, but in general connected
with the wearing of undyed garments of wool (sūf). At first it was
not a uniform but a mark of personal penitence, and some early
ascetics condemned the use of it. Ibn Sīrīn (d. 729) criticized some
ascetics for wearing sūf 'in imitation of Jesus' (as he said): 'I prefer
to follow the example of the Prophet who dressed in cotton.' It
appears that a particular group of ascetics of Kūfa in the second
century were called generally al-Sūfīya. But by the fourth century
the wearing of woollen garments had become the regular badge of
the Sūfis of Iraq and the name was commonly applied to all mystics.
The suggestion that the name was derived from the Greek Sophos or
Sophia seems to be quite fanciful.

In the second century, the first traces of collective organization
appear in small groups for pious discussion and also the first con-
vents, collections of cells imitated from the Melkite hermitages, or

of grottoes in imitation of the Nestorians. Groups of ascetics met for
the purpose of reciting aloud the Koran and other religious pieces,
and these recitations gradually took on a liturgical character (*dhikr*),
evolving in the direction of 'spiritual concerts' (*samā'*) with their
attendant perils of ecstatic fervours. Of the later developments of the
dhikr more will be said in due course, but already al-Hallāj found it
necessary to condemn the revivalist element which it contained:

It is Thou that castest me into ecstasy, not the *dhikr*;
Far from my heart be the thought of cleaving to my *dhikr*;
The *dhikr* is the pearl of the throatpiece which hides Thee from my eyes.

At the same time a change was coming over the general character
of this asceticism. At first its basis was fear of God and of the Wrath
to come, the same fear that had inspired Mohammed; and the
mystical element of love and adoration, if not entirely absent, was
secondary and unstressed. But already in the sayings of the woman
saint, Rābi'a al-Adawīya (d. 801) the mainspring of mysticism is love:
'Love of God hath so absorbed me that neither love nor hate of
any other thing remains in my heart.' And in her famous verses
she distinguishes the illuminative from the contemplative life and
prefers the former:

I love Thee with two loves, love of my happiness,
And perfect love, to love Thee as is Thy due.
My selfish love is that I do naught
But think on Thee, excluding all beside;
But that purest love, which is Thy due,
Is that the veils which hide Thee fall, and I gaze on Thee,
No praise to me in either this or that,
Nay, Thine the praise for both that love and this.

In the end it was this mystical love, so close in its conceptions and
language to the primitive Christian mysticism, which reduced the
ascetic motive of fear to the second place, and supplied the basis
for Sūfism.

This change in the character of Islamic mysticism is associated
also with a change in its leadership. At first the leaders were themselves of the class of Ulamā, or orthodox religious teachers. But in
the course of the third century their place was taken by men who

had not been brought up in the traditional religious disciplines, but who belonged for the most part to the lower middle or artisan classes of the towns, especially from the mixed half-Persian, half-Aramaized Arab population of Baghdad. At the same time, too, certain implications of a social character began to enter into what had been hitherto exclusively—and still remained primarily—a religious movement. While avoiding the political revolutionary aims of the Shi'ite propagandists, it implied a protest none the less against the social and political abuses which appeared to be condoned by the official Sunni Ulamā; but its programme of reform was bound up with the awakening of the religious conscience of individuals and the consequent reaction of this spiritual revival on the social organization of the Community. These social implications were probably reinforced by the labours of the Sūfis in preaching to and converting members of their own class, as well as their missionary labours in other fields. For at all times and in all countries the ascetics and Sūfis were the most active propagandists of Islam.

For both these reasons, the gradual breaking away from orthodox control and the new social implications, the Sūfi movement began to be regarded with suspicion by the orthodox Ulamā and the authorities, and still more by the Shi'a. This suspicion grew as the Sūfi leaders became more 'advanced' in their views and bolder in giving expression to them, and the rift seemed to be widening between Sūfism and orthodoxy. Some attempts were made to silence them; when these failed, an example was made of the most prominent of them, a wool-carder, Mansūr al-Hallāj, who was charged with heresy in having identified himself with God and cruelly executed at the beginning of the fourth century. And it is pertinent to observe that this punishment was inflicted not by violent fanatics but by pious upholders of the ancient faith like the 'Good Wazir', Alī ibn Isā.

Repression, however, proved futile. The Sūfi movement was, for one thing, too firmly based on the Koran and the moral teachings of Islam to be easily put down. Despite the views of some advanced leaders, despite a tendency towards neglect of the ritual prescriptions of Islam, despite even the outside influences which ran counter to the traditional outlook of Islam, its strength lay in the satisfaction which it gave to the religious instincts of the people, instincts which were to some extent chilled and starved by the abstract and impersonal teachings of the orthodox and found relief in the more directly personal and emotional religious approach of the Sūfis. It is essential to bear in mind this popular character and appeal of Sūfism, which arose out of the ranks of the people and appealed to the people, whose main reading-matter, then as even now, was furnished by short lives of the 'saints', often filled out with miraculous works. 'The labours of the mystics and the *qussās* among them were what gave to Islam its permanent type as we know it today. Their spontaneous movement . . . was the first apologetic and categetic of Islam.'[1]

During the fourth and fifth centuries, therefore, it grew in strength, though still frowned upon by the Ulamā, and correspondingly developed more marked congregational features. It was about this time that the *dhikr* and *samā'*, from being simple congregational recitation of and meditation over the Koran, began to show a more definite liturgical tendency, marked especially by the recitation of chants and litanies. It was not this in itself, however, which marked if off from the orthodox services, since similar liturgical ceremonies were commonly performed at that time in the mosques as well. The hostility of the theologians was due partly to the fear that the Sūfi *dhikr* might come to rival or even supplant the mosque as the centre of religious life. At bottom there was a deeper reason for the conflict.

The claims of the theologians to religious leadership were based on their exclusive possession of the sciences of theology and law, and their position as the sole authoritative exponents of Islamic doctrine. It was, as we have seen, after infinite trouble and difficulty that these sciences had been built up, and their acquisition involved long and arduous study. It was by their means that the substance of the Faith had been preserved against both heretical 'innovations' in doctrine and the attempts of the secular arm to override its privileges and obligations. The theologians were justly proud of their system and jealous for the maintenance of its authority. By this

---

[1] D. B. Macdonald in *Encyclopaedia of Islam,* s.v. Kissa.

method alone, they held, could knowledge of the Truth or reality of things be apprehended and preserved, and any relaxation would open the way to heresy and corruption, both spiritual and material. These claims, however, were bluntly and even derisively rejected by the Sūfis. There was, in *their* view, but one way to knowledge —not the rational and second-hand 'knowledge' (*'ilm*) of the schools, but direct and personal 'experience' (*ma'rifa*) culminating in momentary union or absorption into the Godhead. Theology, so far from assisting this process, actually hindered it. The conflict between doctrinaire legist and follower of the Inner Light was fundamental and seemed irreconcilable.

It would take too long to review all the outside influences and doctrines which were finding their way into Sūfism during these formative centuries. Two instances will suffice. True Koranic asceticism condemned celibacy: 'Ye that are unmarried shall marry' is the plain command given in the Koran (xxiv, 32). Christian asceticism on the other hand condemned marriage, but in face of the whole spirit of Islam could not effect a reversal of Muslim doctrine. Nevertheless, it steadily gave currency to traditions ascribed to Mohammed in which the old ascetic denunciation of women reappears. Gradually it began to influence Sūfi practice; while in the third century practically all Sūfis were married, by the fifth we find one of the main exponents of Sūfism writing: 'It is the unanimous opinion of the leaders of this doctrine that the best and most distinguished Sūfis are the unmarried, if their hearts are unstained and their minds free from sin and lust.'[1]

The other doctrine, which was scarcely less fateful for the future of Islam than the exaltation of Mohammed, was the veneration accorded by the disciple to his Sūfi shaikh during his life and the elevation of former shaikhs to the rank of saints. Nothing could be more foreign to primitive Islamic ideas; but in the teeth of the Koran, Tradition, rationalism, and orthodox theology (which regarded the invocation of saints as trespassing into polytheism by derogating from the worship of God alone) the worship of saints crept into the Islamic fold and eventually swept everything before it. 'Know (says the same authority) that the principle and founda-

[1] Al-Hujwīri, *Kashf al-Mahjūb*, tr. R. A. Nicholson, p. 363.

tion of Sūfism and knowledge of God rests on Saintship.'[1] But with saint-worship came another Christian-Gnostic doctrine, scarcely less repugnant to orthodoxy: the belief in the existence of a saintly hierarchy culminating in the *Qutb*, the Pole of the world, who with his saintly vicegerents and hosts governs and superintends the earth, the old Demiourgos in an Islamic dress. And to this day the visitor to the Zuwēla Gate in Cairo will find it covered with shreds of cloth attached to the nails in the door by pious suppliants of the Qutb.

So far, then, from diminishing and disappearing, as time went on, under the influence of the opposition of the Muslim doctors, these popular non-Islamic elements established themselves more and more firmly with the Islamic fold. More and more the pedantry of the orthodox schools drove the religious-minded into the ranks of the mystics, where men sought not metaphysical 'knowledge' of religion but living 'experience' of God. During the fifth century there was a marked drift towards Sūfism of some of the ablest thinkers and a search for some principle of compromise, which prepared the way for the revolution that seemed to come with startling suddenness about the end of the same century. A striking symptom of this change of attitude was given by the treatise of a celebrated theologian al-Qushairi (d. 1072) in which he urged the cause of the higher Sūfism and the acceptance of the Sūfi doctrine of ecstatic communion with the divine.

But the name with which the revolution is linked is that of al-Ghazāli (d. 1111), a man who stands on a level with Augustine and Luther in religious insight and intellectual vigour. The story of his religious pilgrimage is a fascinating and instructive one—how he found himself in revolt against the casuistry of the theologians and set out to seek the ultimate Reality through all the Muslim religious systems and philosophies of his time, and how at length, after a long struggle, bodily, mental and intellectual, he fell back in sheer philosophic agnosticism on personal experience of God and found it in the Sūfi path.

Al-Ghazāli's work and influence has been summed up by Professor Macdonald in a classic passage:

[1] Al-Hujwīri, *Kashf al-Mahjūb*, tr. R. A. Nicholson, p. 210.

First, he led men back from scholastic labours upon theological dogmas to living contact with, study and exegesis of, the Word and the traditions. What happened in Europe when the yoke of medieval scholasticism was broken happened in Islam under his leadership.

Second, in his teaching and moral exhortations he reintroduced the element of fear. It was no time, he held, for smooth, hopeful preaching. The horrors of hell must be kept before men; he had felt them himself.

Third, it was by his influence that Sūfism attained a firm and assured position in the Church of Islam.

Fourth, he brought philosophy and philosophical theology within the range of the ordinary mind.

Of these four phases of al-Ghazāli's work, the first and the third are undoubtedly the most important. He made his mark by leading Islam back to its fundamental and historical facts, and by giving a place in its system to the emotional religious life. He was not a scholar who struck out a new path, but a man of intense personality who entered on a path already blazed and made it the common highway.[1]

The life-work of al-Ghazāli bears a striking analogy to that of al-Ash'ari. Both of them, at a time when orthodoxy was in conflict with another current of thought which strongly attracted the minds and wills of religious thinkers, forged a synthesis that allowed the essential principles of the other movement to find accommodation in the orthodox system. Al-Ash'ari, having been a Mu'tazilite, was able to reinforce orthodox Islam by putting its theology on a logical basis. Al-Ghazāli, having been an Ash'arite theologian, was able to re-establish theology on a basis of personal mystical experience. For it must not be thought that, in adopting the Sūfi 'path', he rejected his former theology; it is rather that the certainties of personal experience allowed him to combine with great boldness and confidence, what had hitherto seemed separate and conflicting scholastic, philosophical, and mystical systems of ideas.

Furthermore, just as, in the case of Ash'arism, the new body of ideas once absorbed, developed within the orthodox fold as an integral element of Muslim thought and went far to transform its nature, so now the 'way' of the mystics, stamped with the approval

[1] D. B. Macdonald, *Development of Muslim Theology,* pp. 238–9. I have abridged the original text.

of *ijmā'* and accepted as orthodox, opened a new stage in the history
of Muslim religious development. And (as had happened with
Ash'arism also) some of the directions taken in the course of this
development were unexpected and disconcerting.

This was not merely because of the logical incompatibility of
Sūfism with Ash'arite theology in the last resort. The oriental
thinker, though he is apt to press an argument to conclusions by
what seems to us an excessive reliance on the method of logical
deduction, is not disturbed by inconsistencies between the conclusions so derived from accepted postulates. With his habitual distrust
of human reason, he is content to accept them as each standing for
a facet of ultimate truth, which can be completely synthesized only
in the Divine mind. More important was the fact that orthodoxy and
mysticism had tended to follow diverging paths: now, although they
were tied to one another, their paths remained separate. This was
fraught with grave consequences. Orthodoxy, however austere and
scholastic, had always maintained high moral and intellectual
standards, and refused to countenance (in matters of religious belief
and practice) innovations and usages which detracted from the
purity of early doctrine. Though it had borrowed the weapon of
Greek dialectic, it had used it on the whole in order to maintain its
positions against Greek ideas. But this had a weak side in giving it
a rather aristocratic or exclusive character, to some extent removed
from the understanding and hearts of the people.

Sūfism, in spite of the loftiness of its religious ideals, had almost
from the first been less fastidious and more ready to admit alien
practices and ideas provided that they seemed to produce results.
Within the ranks of the mystics there were wide gradations, ranging
from men of great intellectual attainments and character to whom
mysticism offered a rich spiritual experience, strengthening their
grasp of the truths of their religion, down to those who found in
mysticism an emotional and moral satisfaction and cared little
whether their practices and postulates were in harmony or not with
Islamic doctrine. Already in some circles the pursuit of the ecstatic
state had affected the primitive *dhikr* and introduced into its ritual
such adventitious aids as dancing and the rending of garments. The
leaders of Sūfism had regarded with some indulgence this influx of

elements of popular religion, though they may perhaps have hoped that, by a closer association with orthodoxy, the practice of Sūfism would itself be purified from these doubtful accretions.

The first results were, indeed, promising. The orthodox church was undoubtedly refreshed and strengthened, and acquired a more popular character and a new power of attraction. During the century after al-Ghazāli it won over large sections of the population in Western Asia and North Africa which had hitherto held somewhat aloof. Shi'ism in particular seems to have suffered an eclipse, and lost much of its influence, except in a few mountain fastnesses and the fringes of the Persian Gulf. It was not only in the old Muslim lands that these effects were seen; in the vast new areas (Asia Minor, Central Asia, India, Indonesia, and Central Africa) which were in process of annexation to the Islamic dominions, multitudes were brought over to Islam in spite of wide and old-standing differences of religious outlook.

But there were features even in this mass movement which were received with misgiving by the stricter Ulamā. What al-Ghazāli did not foresee (and cannot be held responsible for) was that through the breach which he made there would rush in a full tide of popular religious practices and of heterodox intellectual conceptions by which his ideals would be debased and the orthodox doctrines of Islam gravely disturbed. For this acceptance of Sūfism could not be limited to a simple compromise; now that Sūfism itself was orthodox, it was impossible to hold to the old hard and fast lines which had been drawn between what was and what was not permissible and which had set a barrier to the penetration of the popular practices. The compromise became a capitulation; Sūfism swept over the whole body of Islam and rode roughshod over, though it could not entirely stifle, the resistance of the scholastic theologians. The very success of the Sūfi missionaries was probably one of the main reasons for their acquisition of such a height of prestige and such a measure of secular support that it became an almost hopeless task for the theologians to attempt to stem the popular tide. This was markedly seen in the attitude of the Turkish rulers (such, for example, as Timur) who were outwardly respectful to the Ulamā, but positively humble before the Sūfi shaikhs.

Before matters came to this pass, however, the orthodox set themselves to the task of meeting the challenge. The earlier struggle
against Greek influences and the heretical sects had shown the
theologians the value of organizing and controlling higher education. Until the middle of the fifth century, education had been provided for in an unsystematic and on the whole private way. The
mosque served as centre of instruction and every scholar who had
perfected himself in some branch or other of religious studies became
the centre of a group of students, to whom he in due course issued
an *ijāza,* or authorization to teach to others what they had learned
from him. The beginnings of systematic education seem to be connected with the struggle against Shi'ism, which had taken the
initiative in establishing regular schools (e.g. al-Azhar, founded by
the Fātimid governor in the new city of Cairo in 969). Towards the
end of the fifth century a movement began in Persia and spread
westwards for the establishment and endowment of *madrasas,* or
institutions for theological instruction, with an official status,
salaried teachers, and in many institutions also provision for the
maintenance of students as well. Within the next two or three centuries hundreds of these madrasas were set up throughout the eastern
Islamic lands and in Egypt, and brought the control of higher
education more and more into the hands of the theologians.

In these institutions the upper classes and all the educated elements
received a grounding in the traditional disciplines and fundamental
doctrines and principles of Islam, which served, though necessarily
within a relatively limited sphere, to counteract the antinomian
tendencies and laxity manifested in several of the Sūfi groups. By
this means there was created in every country an influential body of
men, who had the task of leading the half-converted masses gradually into the orthodox fold. Nevertheless, we must admit that this
control often had what appeared to us to have been serious results
for the future of Islam. Originality and vitality were gradually
crushed out of existence, the field of study was restricted except
among a favoured few, to a narrowing circle of traditional subjects
acquired by rote and endlessly reproduced in lifeless commentaries.
The theology of Islam as taught in the madrasas remained in the
grip of the dead hand, so going far to give colour to the charge of

petrified medievalism which has been laid against the Ulamā almost down to our own day.

Though there is a measure of truth in this charge, it does some injustice to the Ulamā at the same time. A fully developed theology is not lightly to be changed or set aside, nor can it be, so long as it meets the needs of the community which it serves. It may at most be restated in terms of the changing thought-forms of the community. From the thirteenth to the nineteenth century no new currents of thought entered into the Islamic community to stimulate intellectual speculation, partly because it had attained a measure of internal equilibrium, and partly because it was isolated from the influence of the Western Renaissance. Not that, as it is sometimes supposed, these were centuries of complete intellectual stagnation, for within the community the conflict of Sūfi monism or pantheism with orthodox theology remained a live issue. How strong the challenge of the Sūfi theology became will be seen in the next chapter. It was this challenge that set the terms of the activity of the Ulamā. While popular religion was running to seed in extravagant forms of theosophy, their task was to furnish the sheet-anchor which would hold the community fast to the essentials of Islamic belief and maintain its unity. Their action can not unfairly be compared to the stand made by the Christian Church in the Dark Ages and it deserves the same recognition.

9
The Sūfi Orders

It was suggested in the preceding chapter that the rigidity of orthodox theology, as it was taught in the madrasas or seminaries, can be
to some extent justified by the inner conflict with Sūfism. Under
the genial influence of recognition, certain tendencies which had
always existed in Sūfi thought developed with startling rapidity. At
the same time, from a discipline confined to small and free associations of adepts, Sūfism expanded into a network of organizations
that spread from end to end of the Muslim world, with their own
hierarchies, rituals, and schools.

The early Sūfis, in their pursuit of mystical experience, had
elaborated a series of 'stages' which, with their ascetic moral
disciplines, corresponded to the Christian 'purgative way'. A typical
example of such a series is: repentance, abstinence, renunciation,
poverty, patience, trust in God, satisfaction. From the time of al-
Hallāj (see p. 91) some influential Sūfi groups had begun to combine with these practical disciplines ideas derived from gnostic or
Plotinian doctrine. This philosophical tendency was reinforced
during the two centuries between al-Hallāj and al-Ghazāli by the
diffusion of the *Epistles of the Pure Brethren,* an encyclopaedia of
popularized Neoplatonist natural philosophy which originated in
Ismal'ili or extreme Shi'ite circles. Under its influence the former
purgative stages were related to a ladder of ascending degrees of
'absorption'—human nature, angelic nature, power, divinity. The
initiate retraces the stages of cosmic evolution until he 'rebecomes'
God.

Although the Neoplatonist ideas and vocabulary occupy a prominent place in the works of al-Ghazāli, they are still subordinated to the old Koranic structure of ideas with its purely Muslim terminology. But little more than a century later all the speculative elements that had entered into Sūfi thought were elaborated into a new eclectic system by the Spanish-Arabic writer, Ibn al-Arabi of Murcia (d. at Damascus 1240). In view of the bulk of his writings and the unreconciled contradictions which they contain, it is not easy to pin down his ideas with precision. But that his system as a whole is outspokenly monist and pantheistic cannot be denied. While he appeals to orthodox texts and authorities, he explains away or glosses over whatever is opposed to his philosophy, and his commentary on the Koran is a *tour de force* of esoteric interpretation.

To the orthodox theologians Ibn al-Arabi was little better than an infidel, but his works exercised a powerful attraction throughout the Eastern Islamic world, especially in the Persian and Turkish zones. The mystical interpretation of Islamic doctrine which he claimed to have been revealed to himself as the 'Seal of the Saints' became a rival intellectual system to that of the orthodox theology. This was grave enough, but even graver perhaps was its influence on the leaders of the Sūfi movement. The schools of mystics became closed circles of initiates, and the emphasis was shifted from moral self-control to metaphysical knowledge with its sequence of psychological ascent to the 'Perfect Man', the microcosm in whom the One is manifested to Himself. By no means all Sūfis, of course, were drawn into this pantheistic religion, and little of it percolated through to the great body of devout Muslims who adhered to the major Orders, at least; yet it opened the door to those aberrations and compromises which the Sūfi movement was subsequently to cover with its authority.

A characteristic feature of the literary expression of this later Sūfism is its adoption (following the example set also by Ibn al-Arabi) of the language of earthly love and passion to express ecstatic communion with the divine love. The language used is often so much anthropomorphic realism that even Muslim scholars have sometimes expressed doubts—as, for example, in regard to the odes of the Persian poet Hāfiz—whether the poet is describing the joys of earthly or of divine love.

But the chief presentations of pantheistic Sūfism are to be found in the mystical poems of the great Persian Sūfis, and especially Jalāl ad-Dīn ar-Rūmi and Jāmi. Thus Jāmi says:

> The Eye of the Beloved, seeing what was not, regarded nonentity as existent.
> Although he beheld His attributes and qualities as a perfect whole in His own Essence,
> Yet He desired that they should be displayed to Him in another mirror
> And that each one of His eternal attributes should become manifest accordingly in a diverse form.
> Therefore He created the verdant fields of Time and Space and the life-giving garden of the World,
> That every branch and leaf and fruit might show forth His various perfections.[1]

Elsewhere he puts the same idea into more philosophical language (derived from Ibn al-Arabi):

> The Unique Substance viewed as absolute . . . is the Real [al-Haqq]. On the other hand, viewed in His aspect of multiplicity and plurality, under which He displays himself when clothed with phenomena, He is the whole created universe. Therefore the universe is the outward visible expression of the Real, and the Real is the inner unseen reality of the Universe. The Universe before it was evolved to outward view was identical with the Real, and the Real after this evolution is identical with the Universe.

The new social evolution of Sūfism also owed something to this intellectual development. If there was a doctrine to be learned, it had to be taught in some organized fashion. Already al-Ghazāli had laid it down that

> the disciple [murīd] must of necessity have recourse to a director [shaikh, or in Persian pīr] to guide him aright. For the way of the Faith is obscure, but the Devil's ways are many and patent, and he who has no shaikh to guide him will be led by the Devil into his ways. Wherefore the disciple must cling to his shaikh as a blind man on the edge of a river clings to his leader, confiding himself to him entirely, opposing him in no matter whatsoever, and binding himself to follow him absolutely. Let

---

[1] R. A. Nicholson, *The Mystics of Islam*, p. 81.

him know that the advantage he gains from the error of his shaikh, if he should err, is greater than the advantage he gains from his own rightness, if he should be right.

Thus, out of the originally loose and voluntary associations, there grew up, as Sūfism swelled into a popular movement, organized brotherhoods of 'poor men' or 'mendicants' (Arabic *faqīr*, pl. *fuqarā*; Persian *darwīsh*). Pious men of outstanding personality, reputed to be blessed with the gift of miraculous powers or even of creation *ex nihilo*, found disciples crowding to them. A simple initiation ceremony was evolved or taken over from the initiation ceremony of the Shi'ite or Qarmati guilds, in which the disciple formally pledged devotion. Thereafter he lived in close association with his shaikh or *pīr*, until he reached the higher stages of initiation, when he might go out to teach his master's 'way' (*tarīqa*) in his turn to new disciples in another centre.

The master's residence became in this way the centre of a *darwīsh* community, and regular monasteries (*ribāt*, Persian *khāngāh*) were established, endowed by the pious gifts of adherents and supporters, so that both shaikhs and disciples might have no need to engage in secular occupations, but devote themselves to pious exercises and meditation. Initiates who left the founder's monastery often founded daughter monasteries, and from a single centre a chain of affiliated institutions spread far and wide, linked by ties of reverence, obedience, and common ritual to the original shaikh or *pīr*. On the death of the original founder (who was, of course, venerated as a saint) one of his disciples succeeded to the headship of the community, now become a definite religious order, comparable to the monastic orders in Christendom. This successor (called *Khalīfa*, or *Walī al-Sajjāda*, 'inheritor of the [master's] prayer-carpet'; in Persian *Sajjādeh-nishīn*) was either elected, or, in orders where celibacy was not one of the rules, the succession was hereditary in the founder's family.

From the twelfth and thirteenth centuries such orders began to spread their network over the whole Islamic world. Their primitive purpose of guiding beginners in the 'Path' or 'Way' was still indicated by the name of *tarīqa*, but *tarīqas* varied to some extent in degree of organization. Some were organized in an elaborate ascending scale of hierarchy, with hundreds of thousands of followers and adherents, some retained the looser organization or more primitive Sūfism, but the main differences between them lay in their ritual and litany (*dhikr*), and in their characteristic religious attitude, according to whether they were more or less attached to orthodox obervances, tolerant or militant, and so on. Membership was as a rule of two kinds: a higher class of initiates and disciples engaged in religious duties in the monasteries and in the collection of revenues, and a large body of 'lay-members' attached to the order and meeting on stated occasions for the *dhikr*, but otherwise carrying on their secular occupations in village or town.

The organization of these orders constitutes one of the most interesting developments in the history of Islam. In recruitment and appeal they were essentially popular movements; and they were popular movements mainly because the Sūfi missionaries, impatient of the rigid dogmatism of the orthodox scholars, eased the way to conversion (for the common view that the 'simplicity' of Islam exercises in itself a strong appeal over-simplifies the facts). At the same time, this weakening in dogmatic integrity was certain to produce serious consequences. Just as Sūfism had made its way originally by taking up into Islam many older elements of practice and belief in Western Asia, so now the *darwīsh* orders showed an extreme pliability, and even a dangerous readiness to compromise with old religious beliefs and customs in other lands, and to tolerate them provided only that outward adhesion to the Muslim creed was secured.

The effect of all this was to change the general aspect of Islam to a remarkable degree. Whereas down to the twelfth century the Muslim Community was a relatively small homogeneous body (even allowing for doctrinal schisms), it has since embraced about one-seventh of the entire population of the world, but at the same time has become a body which presents in regard to religious beliefs and practices a wide range of differences, not concealed by common acceptance of certain rituals and doctrinal expressions or by the common activities of clerics and lawyers. The popular forms of Islam differ from one another in almost every Muslim country, and often stand in strong contrast to the rigid system of the orthodox Ulamā. On the other hand, the Ulamā have continued to furnish the unifying religious element throughout the whole body, and have patiently striven to educate the newly converted or semi-converted elements in the fundamental principles of the Faith.

But again, amongst the orders themselves, there were marked differences in their relations with the orthodox church. One particularly significant line of cleavage was that between 'urban' orders founded and maintained by elements of the city populations which were in fairly close association with the Ulamā and the madrasas, and 'rustic' orders, which spread chiefly in the villages, and being less open to their influence were liable to diverge more widely from the strict tenets of orthodoxy. As regards their relations with the Shi'a, there are strong traces of their original connexion with early Shi'ism both in the fact that the spiritual lineage of the Sūfi saints is carried back to early Shi'ite figures (such as Salmān 'the Persian') and thence to the Caliph Ali and the Prophet himself, and still more from the underlying assumption that the gnosis, or apprehension of secret spiritual knowledge peculiar to the order, is derived directly from the secret knowledge communicated to Ali by the Prophet. On the other hand, dogmatic Shi'ism as a whole is hostile to the *darwīsh* fraternities, and they are found in consequence almost exclusively among Sunnis. Indeed the wretched and degraded state of the majority of Shi'ite *darwīshes* furnishes a striking measure of the success attained by the Sunni Ulamā in defence of orthodox standards.

The total number of orders or fraternities in the Muslim world is very large, and there is no room here to do more than mention a few examples of different types in different countries and to note briefly some of their special features.

The most typical urban order is that of the *Qādirīya,* named after Abd al-Qādir al-Jīlānī or Gīlānī (1077–1166). Originally a philologist and Hanbali jurist, his popularity as a teacher at Baghdad led to the building of a *ribāt* for him by public subscription outside the gates of the city. His writings are generally orthodox in content, with a tendency to mystical interpretation of the Koran, but the enthusiasm of his later followers credited him with all manner of miracles and claims to pre-eminence in the mystical hierarchy. He is said to have had forty-nine children, of whom eleven sons carried on his work and with other disciples carried his teaching into other parts of Western Asia and Egypt. The head of the order and keeper of the tomb at Baghdad is still a direct descendant. At the end of the nineteenth century there were a vast number of provincial congregations, extending from West Africa to the East Indies, loosely connected to the central institution in Baghdad, which is visited by great numbers of pilgrims every year.

The Qādiri order is on the whole amongst the most tolerant and progressive orders, not far removed from orthodoxy, distinguished by philanthropy, piety, and humility, and averse to fanaticism, whether religious or political. It seems unlikely that the founder instituted any rigid system of devotional exercises, and these in fact differ in the various congregations. A typical *dhikr* is the following, to be recited after the daily prayers: 'I ask pardon of the mighty God; Glorified be God; May God bless our Master Mohammed and his household and Companions; There is no God but Allah', each phrase repeated a hundred times.

The looseness of the Qādirīya favoured the development of numerous sub-orders, some of which have grown into independent organizations. One of the most important of these in Western Asia, the *Rifā'īya,* was founded by al-Jīlānī's nephew Ahmad al-Rifā'i (d. 1182), also in Iraq. This order was distinguished by a more fanatical outlook and more extreme practices of self-mortification, as well as extravagant thaumaturgical exercises, such as glass-eating, fire-walking, and playing with serpents, which have been imputed to the influence of primitive Shamanism during the Mongol occupation of Iraq in the thirteenth century.

During St. Louis's invasion of Egypt in the Seventh Crusade a Rifā'i disciple, the Egyptian Ahmad al-Bedawi (d. 1276), played a notable part in stirring up the population to resist the invaders. The order which he founded, called after him the *Bedawīya* or *Ahmadīya,* is the most popular 'rustic' order in Egypt, and became notorious for the orgies, inherited from early Egyptian practices, which until recent times accompanied the fairs around his tomb at Tanta, in the Delta. The other two popular orders in Lower Egypt, the Bayyūmi and Dasūqi orders, are both offshoots of the Bedawīya.

In North-West Africa, the Sūfi movement developed along peculiar lines and with stronger political connexions. During the first three centuries of Islam, Berber reaction against Arab domination took the form of adhesion to the Khārijite or Shi'ite heresies, but the masses remained strongly attached to their primitive animistic beliefs, especially in the magical powers of 'holy men'. The first native dynasty of more than local importance, the Almoravids (eleventh century) initiated a religious movement on orthodox lines, but they succumbed after a brief period to a new Berber dynasty, the Almohads (twelfth century). Through its spiritual director, the Mahdi Ibn Tūmart, the Ahmohad movement was linked up from the first with the Sūfi movement, and the religious enthusiasm which it generated brought Islamic influences to bear for the first time upon the main body of the Berbers.

The agents in this campaign were mostly local men, often illiterate, whose aim was to attract and convert their fellow-countrymen to the ethical and mystical principles of Eastern Sūfism. Most of them had attached themselves for a time to some celebrated saint in Spain or Egypt, and then returned to their native villages to spread a few simple maxims of religious devotion and renunciation. The most famous is Abū Madyan (d. end of twelfth century) whose whole doctrine was contained in a single verse: 'Say "God", and abandon all that is material or pertains thereto, if thou desirest to attain the true end.'

Four centuries later, Sūfi leadership stimulated the Muslim reaction against Spanish and Portuguese pressure in Morocco. Yet the Berbers remained animists through and through; and the persistence of the old beliefs and practices has given a characteristic feature to Berber Islam, the prevalence of 'Maraboutism' or the cult of living 'holy men', possessing magical powers (baraka).

The Sūfi movement in the Barbary States had a twofold radiation. On the one hand it spread into the Negrolands on the Niger, where (with a similar background of animism) the local marabout (alūfa) replaced the old 'medicine-man' of negro Fetishism. On the other hand, it exercised a powerful influence on Eastern Islam through two outstanding personalities.

One of these was no other than Ibn al-Arabi, the apostle of

pantheistic mysticism. Originally a follower of the puritan Zāhiri school (p. 70), he was initiated into Sūfism by Yūsuf al-Kūmi, a personal disciple of Abū Madyan. The other was al-Shādhili (d. 1258), who had studied in Fez under another disciple of the same master. Al-Shādhili eventually settled in Alexandria, where a circle of pupils gathered round him. He had no monastery and no set forms of ritual, and he discouraged his adherents from giving up their trades and professions for the contemplative life. But little more than a generation later, his disciples adopted the normal organization of a *tarīqa,* which spread over North Africa and into Arabia. The town of Mokha (in the Yemen) in particular adopted al-Shādhili as its patron saint and venerates him as the originator of coffee-drinking.

The *Shādhilīya* order is in general more extravagant in ritual and more ecstatic than the Qādirīya, but is remarkable especially for the large number of sub-orders to which it gave rise, both directly and in conjunction with the Qādirīya. Among the best known are the *Isawīya,* with its famous sword-slashing ritual, and at the other extreme the orthodox and austere *Derqāwā* of Morocco and Western Algeria.

Among the Turks and Mongols also, Muslim propaganda came into close contact with animism, in the form of shamanism, and had to reckon with deeply rooted Turkish customs. The oldest Turkish mystical order, the 'rustic' order of the *Yesevīya,* for example, owed to Turkish custom the unique feature that women took part in the *dhikr* unveiled.

Amongst the Ottoman Turks in Anatolia and Europe the most characteristic order was another 'rustic' order, that of the Bektāshis. This, which was said to be an offshoot of the Yesevis and was fully established at the end of the fifteenth century, was a peculiar synecretism apparently connected on the one side with esoteric Shi'ism and on the other with a good deal of popular Christianity and Gnosticism. The Bektashis went much farther than other orders in regarding the outer ceremonies of Islam as unimportant and negligible; and in their rituals there were some remarkable analogies to those of Christianity. For example, in place of a regular liturgical *dhikr,* they had a sort of communion with the sharing of wine, bread, and cheese, and they also observed the practice of confession to their superiors (*babas*). The Bektāshi order acquired enormous prestige through its association with the Ottoman janissaries, but since their suppression in 1826 it has been gradually declining and now surves only in Albania. The principal 'urban' order amongst the Ottoman Turks was the *Mevleviya,* founded by the famous Persian mystical poet Jalāl ad-Dīn al-Rūmi (d. at Konia 1273), whose *dhikr* was remarkable for the pirouetting exercise of the adepts ('dancing dervishes'). Since the secularization of the Turkish Republic, the Mevlevis are reduced to a few *tekkes* in Aleppo and other towns of the Middle East.

It is, however, in India that popular Islam presents the most bewildering diversity of orders, rituals, and beliefs. In addition to the adherents of the great universal orders (Qādiris, Naqshbandis, etc.) and an important order of the same type which is peculiar to India, the Chishti order (founded by Mu'īn al-Dīn Chishti of Sistan, d. at Ajmir in 1236), each with several sub-divisions, a very large proportion of Indian Muslims are connected with the so-called irregular (*bē-shar'*) orders. These are of all kinds, ranging from less reputable offshoots of the regular orders, through a great variety of independent orders—of which the most famous is the itinerant *Qalandari,* (the 'Calenders' of the *Arabian Nights*)—down to un-organized wandering mendicants or 'faqīrs', who claim to be associated with the shrine of some saint or other. The varieties of beliefs, rituals, customs and so on associated with these irregular orders naturally correspond to their number, and in many cases their connexion with Islam is purely nominal. Hindu and even pre-Hindu customs and tenets (which have influenced even some of the great orders) are more or less predominant in these, and the practices of their members have contributed more than anything else to bring the term *darwīsh* into general disrepute.

Apart from these orders Hindu influences play a preponderating part in the religious life of the illiterate and only partly converted Muslim villagers. Innumerable villages still preserve intact the idolatrous worship of local gods, and demon-worship has left its mark in the respect often paid, particularly amongst women, to the mythical Shaikh Saddū. Cases are recorded in the Mughal period of suttee amongst Muslims, and there are several communities which keep up the ritual of the sacred fire. Even caste has found its way into Indian Islam. The position was summed up thus by one of the leaders of Islam in modern India, Sir Muhammad Iqbāl, himself a mystic:

Is the organic unity of Islam intact in this land? Religious adventurers set up different sects and fraternities, ever quarrelling with one another; and there are castes and sub-castes like the Hindus. Surely we have out-Hindued the Hindu himself; we are suffering from a double caste system —the religious caste system, sectarianism, and the social caste system, which we have either learned or inherited from the Hindus. This is one of the quiet ways in which the conquered nations revenge themselves on their conquerors.[1]

Despite all the services of the more high-principled orders, the tendency to resort to extravagant methods of auto-hypnosis and to compromise with traditional animistic practices not only opened the way to charlatanism, but lowered the moral standards of the greater part of the Muslim community. In so far as Sūfism was represented by the wandering and often ill-balanced *darwīsh,* it became a clog on their social and religious life. But so strong was the pull it exerted that the opposition of the Ulamā gradually weakened, in spite of the vigorous resistance of a few outstanding figures, such as Ibn Taimīya (d. 1328), who condemned saint-worship and Sūfi practices and theology root and branch.

In Western Asia the Sūfi movement reached its climax with the establishment of the Ottoman Empire in the sixteenth century. It would seem that every village and every trade-guild and class in the cities was affiliated to one or other of the orders, and even the antinomian *Melāmīya*[2] had its followers in the higher ranks of the administration. The only way by which the Ulamā could hope to maintain the balance between orthodoxy and Sūfism was to reform Sūfism from within. Their enrolment led to a considerable revival and extension of the more orthodox orders, especially the

[1] Quoted by Murray Titus, *Indian Islam,* p. 171.
[2] These were adepts who affected an outward disregard for religion and morality, and engaged in religious exercises in private. Cf. al-Hujwīri, tr. R. A. Nicholson, pp. 62–9.

Naqshbandīya (originally founded in Central Asia in the fourteenth century and now propagated from India) and the Anatolian order of *Khalwatīya,* propagated in Egypt and Syria in the eighteenth century by Shaikh Mustafā al-Bakri (d. 1749).

This fresh infusion of Sūfism could not fail to leave its mark on the structure of religious thought and orthodox education. During the seventeenth and eighteenth centuries a succession of remarkable scholars strove to restate the bases of Islamic theology in a manner which broke away from the formalism of the orthodox manuals and laid new stress upon the psychological and ethical elements in religion. Among the more outstanding figures in this movement, which has not yet received the attention it deserves, were the Syrian Abd al-Ghani of Nāblus (1641–1731), and the Indians Ahmad Sarhindi (1563–1624) and Shah Walī-Allāh of Delhi (1702–62).

Even among the Shi'ite divines of Persia, in spite of strong opposition, the influence of Sūfi ideas was not wholly eliminated. The official establishment of the Shi'ite doctrine by the new Safavid rulers in the sixteenth century had of course stimulated the production of a formal scholastic literature, both in Persian and in Arabic, on Shi'ite religious topics, the results of which were authoritatively summed up in the works of Mohammed Bāqir Majlisi (d. 1699). But alongside this, the earlier flowering of Sūfi poetry in Persia and the doctrines of Ibn al-Arabi continued to exercise an attraction which no theological condemnations could uproot.

Among the more general doctrines was that of a 'world of similitudes' (*'ālam al-mithāl*), a world of images or metaphysical realm in which the gross bodies from the material realm from below are changed by the substitution of subtle bodies or images. In the writings of the philosopher Mohammed Sadr ad-Dīn (Mullā Sadrā, d. 1640), the human spirit can attain to the different levels corresponding to those of the *'ālam al-mithāl* and thus gain freedom from the finite existence of the material world. This influenced the development of a new Shi'ite heterodoxy called, after its systematizer Shaikh Ahmad of al-Ahsā (d. 1826), the *Shaikhīya*. Little as the real character and doctrines of this sect are known, there is an unmistakable point of resemblance with the 'world of similitudes' and the contemporary orthodox Sūfism. The principal doctrine of the

Shaikhis, however, seems to have been the necessity for a living channel of communication with the 'Hidden Imām', and this was the root from which the Bābi movement sprang in the nineteenth century.

10
Islam in the Modern World

To AN observer at the end of the eighteenth century it might well have appeared that the historical evolution of Islam had reached its term. From the simple, rigid, and austere monotheism preached by Mohammed to a small Arab community it had broadened into an intricate complex of legal schools and theological sects, superimposed on a medley of congregations with their own rituals and an extra-ordinary diversity of religious ideas and practices. And if our observer's outlook were coloured by the contemporary philosophy of Western Europe, he might well have regarded the whole structure as seamed with superstition and destined to be swept away before long by the forces of progress and enlightenment.

But no outside observer can estimate the strength of those unseen threads which at an hour of challenge draw the members of diverse groups into a single community of purpose and will, nor the vitality of a great idea, overlaid by the deposits of long centuries, when it is faced with new tasks and dangers. The history of Islam in the nineteenth and twentieth centuries is a history of revival and efforts at readjustment under the double stimulus of challenge from within and pressing dangers from without. Slowly at first, and not without setbacks but with increasing momentum, the Muslim community has gathered itself together and begun to look to its defences; re-awakened and alert, it is searching for the programme with which to advance united into an unknown and unpredictable future.

In the eyes of most Muslims and almost all Westerners, the external pressures arising from the political and economic expansion of Western Europe loom much larger than the internal challenge. But the latter came first and from the heart of the Muslim society; and its effects may well be much more profound than those which have resulted from the impact of the West.

Its starting-point was Central Arabia where, about the year 1744, a certain Mohammed ibn Abd al-Wahhāb opened, with the support of the House of Su'ūd, the local emirs of Dar'īya, a revivalist campaign based on the puritan Hanbalite school and the anti-Sūfi polemic of Ibn Taimīya and his followers in the fourteenth century. Directed in the first instance against the laxity of manners and corruption of religion in the local settlements and tribes, the Wahhābi movement (as it came to be known) condemned saint-worship and all the other Sūfi 'innovations' as heresy and infidelity, and finally attacked the other orthodox schools as well for their compromises with these abominations. In their zeal to restore the primitive purity of the Faith, the Su'ūdi princes took up arms against their neighbours, and, after conquering Central and Eastern Arabia, turned them against the Ottoman provinces in the north and the hereditary Sharīfs of Mecca in the Hijāz. Kerbelā in Iraq was sacked in 1802, Mecca finally captured, occupied, and 'purified' in 1806. With this double challenge to the Ottoman power and to the catholic tradition of Islam, the Wahhābis, hitherto an obscure sect, drew the eyes of the whole Muslim world. The challenge was taken up on behalf of the Sultan by the governor of Egypt, Mohammed Ali, and by 1818 the Wahhābi power was broken, Dar'īya captured and razed, and the reigning Su'ūdi sent to execution at Constantinople.

But this eclipse of its political power in Arabia did not mean the end of the Wahhābi movement. Even on the political plane, its effects were too enduring to be easily uprooted. A Su'ūdi emirate lingered on in Nejd, and though overshadowed for a time by its former vassals of the House of Rashīd in Hā'il, it renewed its strength and regained an Arabian empire in the present century under the leadership of Abd al-Azīz, the creator of the new Kingdom of 'Saudi Arabia'.

Still more profound has been its influence as a religious force within the Muslim community. The intolerance and the excesses of its first adherents in Arabia, and of those like them in India and West

Africa at the beginning of the nineteenth century, earned indeed the condemnation of the general body of Muslims. But the Wahhābi outbreak was only the extreme expression of a tendency which can be traced in many parts of Islam in the course of the eighteenth century; and with the passing of its actively intolerant phase, its principles reinforced the movement for the return to the pure monotheism of the early Muslim church. This movement, combined with a reaction against Sūfi infiltrations, grew steadily throughout the nineteenth century and has come to constitute, now in one form, now in another, one of the outstanding features of Modern Islam.

It is significant that the revolt originated in the most purely Arab province. In their broadest lines the religious forces that had moulded the development of post-Ghazalian Sūfism were non-Arab: Berber, Persian, Turkish; and though it might be fanciful to relate this to the political subjection of the Arab lands, it is none the less true that their inrush had gone far towards weakening both the predominance of the 'Arab idea' in Islam and the influence of the older Arabic theologians up to and including al-Ghazāli. For many Persians and Turks the *Mathnawi* of Jalāl ad-Dīn ar-Rūmi had replaced the Traditions of the Prophet as commentary on, and interpretation of, the religious and ethical teachings of the Koran; and even the leading Ulamā of the eighteenth century, as we have seen, had combined the heritage of the older learning with the speculative doctrines of the later Sūfis.

The Wahhābi revival was the first reassertion of the 'Arab idea', and it was followed by others, independent in origin. At the end of the same century a massive revindication of al-Ghazāli was issued by a Yemenite scholar, Mohammed al-Murtadā (d. 1790). The introduction of Arabic printing into Egypt in 1828 led to the multiplication and spread of the standard works of medieval theology and revived the prestige of the Egyptian tradition of Arabic scholarship. European orientalism, with its editions of old texts and its researches, contributed both directly and by provoking controversy to the focusing of attention on the early centuries. All of these activities combined to emphasize the distinction between earlier and later Islam, and to discredit, in learned and literary circles, the Persian and Turkish veneer. Thus they prepared the way for that recovery

of Arab initiative and influence in the Muslim world which came
to a head with the Egyptian reformist movement led by Mohammed
Abduh at the turn of the present century.

There was still a long way to go, however, before this point was
reached. The Sūfi impulse of the eighteenth century had not yet
spent its force. In North-West Africa, in particular, it gained fresh
triumphs, when a Berber disciple of the Khalwati order, Ahmad
al-Tījāni, founded in 1781 the *Tijāniya* order. The new order spread
rapidly in the further West and into the Negrolands, where it became
associated with a fanatical and sanguinary campaign of proselytiza-
tion, largely at the expense of the peaceful Qādirīya. In India, in
Central Asia, and in most of the outlying Muslim lands, there were
Sūfi revivals during the nineteenth century, and only in the central
Arab countries and cities does Sūfism appear to have steadily
lost ground.

But among the Sūfis also the orthodox revival seemed to exert a
growing influence. Except in the extremer orders and the 'irregular'
brotherhoods, the more extravagant rituals and practices of earlier
days were gradually dropped, together with much of their speculative theology and pantheistic tendencies. The orthodox Ulamā continued to maintain a steady pressure in this direction. In receding
from their former close association with the orders, they took up
on the whole an intermediate position, rejecting both the fundamentalism of the Wahhābis, with its undercurrents of fanaticism
and intolerance, and the claims of the Sūfi adepts. Holding fast to
the catholic doctrine of *ijmā'*, they asserted (and for the most part
still continue to assert) that, although the worship of saints is
contrary to Islam, reverence for the saints and prayers for their
intercession are lawful.

The moderation and conservatism of the Ulamā was not to the
taste of more active reformers, who have in every generation
founded new societies to propagate their principles. In the early part
of the nineteenth century, the most striking of these newer developments was the formation of reformist missionary congregations on a
strict orthodox basis, but organized on the lines of the Sūfi *tarīqas*.
The originator of this movement was a descendant of the Prophet,
the Moroccan *Sharīf* Ahmad ibn Idrīs (d. 1837). Initiated in his

youth into one of the reformed branches of the Shādhilīya, Ahmad ibn Idrīs settled in Mecca, where his outstanding spiritual, intellectual, and personal gifts attracted a devoted following. It is a disputed question whether he was directly influenced by the Wahhābi revolt, but it is certain that he followed the Hanbalites in rejecting *ijmā'*, beyond that of the first generation of the Companions of Mohammed, and *qiyās* or 'analogy' as a legal method. The Koran and the Sunna alone could be accepted as sources of doctrine and law. Along with this, he taught a number of liturgical prayers, corresponding to the Sūfi *dhikr*; but he rejected entirely the Sūfi doctrine of union with God, substituting for it, as the goal of the mystical life, a mystical union with the spirit of the Prophet.

The new *Muhammadīya tarīqa*, as it was called, had an immediate and striking success. Besides the original *tarīqa* (Idrīsīya) of the founder in Arabia itself (where his descendants for a time exercised political authority in the province of Asīr), several of his disciples established other congregations, on the same or similar foundations. The most influential of these were the *tarīqa* founded by the Algerian Mohammed ibn Ali al-Sunūsi (d. 1859) in Cyrenaica, and that of the Hijazi Mohammed Othmān al-Amīr Ghanī (d. 1853) in East Africa.

The different fortunes of these two offshoots of the Muhammadīya provide a remarkable illustration of the part played by circumstances and opportunity in moulding the development of such orders. All puritan reformist movements, even if peaceful in principle, are by nature liable to adopt violent courses. Having from the outset to expect the hostility of the orthodox religious authorities, they are uncompromising in defence and counter-attack; and where the secular arm is turned against them as well, their opposition, being forced into political channels, becomes a revolutionary movement, directed to the foundation of a new theocratic state. And it must not be overlooked that one effect of the renewed emphasis upon Koran and Sunna in Muslim fundamentalism is to restore to *jihād* 'in the path of God' much of the prominence which, as has been seen in Chapter 4, it held in the primitive Community; whereas in the historic Community the concept of *jihād* had gradually weakened and at length been largely reinterpreted in terms of Sūfi ethics.

The *Amīrghanīya* of Nubia and the Sudan, at grips with the more extreme revolutionary order organized by the 'Mahdi' Mohammed Ahmed (d. 1885), became the defenders of the 'Community' and of submission to the secular authority. The *Sunūsīya* of Cyrenaica, on the other hand, rejected Ottoman claims to suzerainty and built up the militant organization which was needed for its missionary task of converting and controlling the nomads of the Libyan desert. At a later stage, however, when they were confronted with the expansion of the Christian Powers, the 'Senussis' adopted the role of defenders of the Faith, first against French penetration into Equatorial Africa, and subsequently as allies of Turkey against the Italians in Libya and the British in Egypt. Militarily crushed and to all appearances destroyed by the Fascist military régime, the Senussi brotherhood has shown vitality by its almost instantaneous revival on the expulsion of the Italians from Cyrenaica.

But long before the missionary congregations in their remote deserts reacted in characteristic fashion to the penetration of the Western Powers, the political and economic impact of the Christian West had begun to create new tensions among the settled Muslim populations. The continuous expansion of European political power over Muslim territories produced in the first place a psychological unsettlement, the effects of which were reinforced successively by the derangement of their old social and economic structure and the intrusion of Western thought.

The channels through which Western ideas percolated were not only literary and educational, but almost infinite in their variety and complexity, affecting government and politics, military organization, law and its administration, transport, hygiene, commerce, industry, and agriculture. Sooner or later the lives of almost every section of the population were affected to some extent by one or other of these developments. Though Western schools and academies exercised the most direct effect upon the literate classes, the most potent influence, probably, was that of the new daily and periodical press. From small beginnings in the principal centres in the middle of the nineteenth century, almost every part of the Muslim world now has its own output of journals, and the press of Egypt in particular radiates far outside its own boundaries.

Confronted with the penetrating and pervasive power of these Western influences, the Muslim was unable to ignore them; but to relate them to the bases of his own life and thought called for an effort of comprehension and adjustment which he was not yet ready to undertake. Yet without the effort, the outcome could only be conflict and confusion, both external and internal, and made more confusing by the conflicting ideas and purposes within the Western forces themselves. To distinguish the effect from the cause, the secondary and superficial from the essential, the instrument from the motive, the false from the true—all this was a task for which even his Western advisers, when he sought their assistance, were too often inadequate and unreliable guides.

On the religious plane, two ways of meeting the challenge of the West presented themselves. One was to start from the basic principles of Islam and to restate them in the light of the contemporary situation. The other was to start from a selected Western philosophy and to attempt to integrate Muslim doctrine with it. Both ways have been followed, but out of the great variety of conflicting interpretations and cross-currents only a few of the more outstanding can be dealt with here.

The first method must not, to begin with, be confounded with the attitude of the Ulamā in general. For them, there has as yet been no question of 'restatement' in any sense. The theology, law, and practice of the orthodox Community, based on the Koran and the Sunna, as interpreted by the great medieval doctors and confirmed by general consensus, remain binding and unalterable, although, under pressure of irresistible circumstances, some concessions in matters of practice may be temporarily allowed. But even those who set out to restate Islamic doctrine might do so from two very different motives. It might be restated on the one hand to serve the purpose of strengthening the Muslim world against the encroachments of the West, or on the other to serve as a datum-line from which any process of adaptation or assimilation should proceed. The emphasis in the one case would be laid more on the external aspects of Muslim practice and organization, in the other on the fundamental principles of Muslim thought.

In the circumstances, it was only natural that the former should

E

precede the latter. In all Muslim communities the Western invasion produced political reactions, such as those which came to a head in the Indian Mutiny of 1857. These lie outside the scope of this book, except to the extent that they involve specific religious attitudes and positions. But for religious minds the political weakness of Islam was to be explained as the consequence of loss of belief and corruption of practice. Thus the first general reform movement in the nineteenth century took on a dual character. On the religious side, it appealed for purification of religious belief and practice, the raising of intellectual standards, and the extension and modernization of education. On the political side, it aimed at removing the causes of division between Muslims and uniting them in defence of the Faith. The protagonist of both was the Afghan Jamāl al-Dīn (1839–97), whose untiring campaigns throughout the Muslim East powerfully stirred Muslim feeling, and contributed to both the Arābi rising in Egypt and the Persian revolution. He was the founder and inspiration of the Pan-Islamic movement, which sought to unite all Muslim peoples under the Ottoman Caliphate; and though he failed in this, his supreme objective, his influence lives on in the more recent popular movements which combine Islamic fundamentalism with an activist political programme.

Among Jamāl al-Dīn's disciples, however, there was one who had the insight to separate the political from the religious reform and the restatement of Islamic doctrine. This was the Egyptian shaikh Mohammed Abduh (1849–1905), a man of great breadth, independence, and nobility of mind. As a young teacher in al-Azhar, he had tried to introduce a broader and more philosophical conception of religious education, and in later exile he had collaborated with Jamāl al-Dīn in a semi-religious, semi-political journal called *al-Urwa al-Wuthqā*. In 1888 he returned to Egypt, and there, in spite of strong opposition from the conservative Ulamā and political opponents, exerted by his character and his teaching an immense influence upon the new generation, who were finding themselves to some extent alienated by the formalism of al-Azhar.

Like the great medieval scholars, Mohammed Abduh expounded his thought in the form of a Commentary on the Koran, although he did not live to complete it. He was a modernist in the sense that he urged the pursuit of modern thought, confident that in the last resort it could not undermine but only confirm the religious truth of Islam. In relation to the traditional orthodox structure of belief he was no innovator. He was not, like al-Ghazāli, a man who framed the line of synthesis by which a body of ideas hitherto outside the orthodox faith could be incorporated in it or accommodated to it. It is sometimes difficult for an outside observer to see why his teaching was so enthusiastically received and so influential on the one hand and so tenaciously opposed on the other. The explanation seems to be that by restating the rights of reason in religious thought he restored some measure of flexibility to what had become a rigid and apparently petrified system, and allowed the possibility of reformulating doctrine in modern instead of medieval terms.

But any such reformulation is not to be achieved in one or two generations. There is no cause for surprise that little outward progress has been made in this direction, especially when political tensions have created and maintained an atmosphere unfavourable to the calm pursuits of the scholar and the theologian. Thus the immediate results of Mohammed Abduh's activity found expression in two different and opposed tendencies.

On the one hand there has grown up in secular circles a widespread but not explicitly formulated 'modernism', which, while holding to the basic dogmas of Islam, is strongly influenced by Western ideas. In its most advanced forms, modernism tends to become confounded with the movement of secularization which aims at separating Church and State and substituting Western systems of law for the Islamic Sharī'a. The most extreme application of secularist principles has been furnished by the Turkish Republic since the abolition of the Ottoman Caliphate in 1924. But though secularism has its supporters in other Muslim countries, the majority of modernists adopt a much more moderate attitude towards the religious organization and its tradition. Whatever their views on matters of law and politics, their doctrinal position may be summed up as a general rejection of the final authority of the medieval doctors, and a more hesitant assertion of the right of private judgement.

The second consequence was the formation of a religious party which called itself the *Salafīya*, the upholders of the tradition represented by the 'Great Ancestors', the Fathers of the Muslim Community. The Salafis agree ·with the modernists in rejecting the authority of the medieval schools and in accepting Koran and Sunna as the sole authority for religious truth. In this respect, as against the generality of the Ulamā, they are reformists; but as against the modernists they passionately reject any intrusion of Western liberalism and rationalism.

The leader of the Salafi movement was Mohammed Abduh's Syrian disciple Shaikh Rashīd Ridā (1865–1935), the editor of his Koran-Commentary and of the reformist journal *al-Manār*, which eventually gained a wide circulation from Morocco to Java. Under his influence, the movement at first reasserted the Pan-Islamic programme of Jamāl al-Dīn; but when the secular rulers of Turkey turned their backs on the Islamic tradition Rashīd Ridā unreservedly condemned their policy. Like the earlier puritan reformers he was steadily driven back on fundamentalism, and at length recognized and cultivated a relationship of purpose and thought between the Salafīya and the Wahhābīya. In their final doctrinal position, the Salafīya, rejecting the too pronouncedly sectarian mood of the Wahhābis, confess themselves 'Neo-Hanbalites', conservatives claiming the reopening of the 'Gate of *Ijtihād*' (p. 66) and the right of reinterpretation in matters of theology and law.

Possibly, however, the strongest link between Salafi and Wahhābi has been their common hostility to any forms of Sūfism, saint-worship, and animistic 'innovation' detracting from the pure monotheism of the Koran. It is partly this stand which made 'Manār-modernism' a force in all those Muslim countries where the reformers found themselves face to face with the vested interests of saint-worship and the Sūfi Brotherhoods. Discarding the cautious middle-of-the-road attitude of the official Ulamā, it created across national and racial boundaries a new brotherhood of enthusiastic groups, determined to make war equally on internal corruption and external disruption. Though not confined to any one cultural level or economic or social group, it had little following amongst the more educated, and in return suspected them of undue laxity in matters of faith and practice.

Parallel to the Salafi movement, but on a less pronounced doctrinal basis, the most striking development in the Muslim community in recent decades was the rise of new religious societies. These too were, in a sense, restatements of Islamic thought and reassertions of the Islamic conscience in face of the Western intrusion, adapted to different social and educational environments. Thus, in Egypt and the Arab lands the 'Association of Muslim Youth' addressed itself to the same kind of public, and with much the same methods, as the Y.M.C.A., while the 'Muslim Brotherhood' operated at a more popular level. Similar, but independent, associations exist in Pakistan and Indonesia.

Aiming primarily to revive and stimulate religious faith and practice, which might otherwise be submerged in the tides of modern life, the new societies tended to take up, almost of necessity, a political attitude also in defence of the heritage of Islam. Thus they represented, among the urban populations of the settled countries, a twentieth-century adaptation of the nineteenth-century movements amongst the tribesmen, and at the same time replaced the older Sūfi orders, whose influence in the cities declined with the break-up of the trade guilds. Embracing all gradations of doctrine from fundamentalism to liberal orthodoxy, they found a common rallying-point in an enthusiastic veneration for the person of the Prophet, which may be said to furnish the chief emotional and ethical stimulus in modern Islam.

The second type of reaction to the Western impact found expression almost exclusively in India. Behind it also, however, lies the influence of the orthodox reform movement, which prepared the way by eliminating the authority of the medieval 'schools'. Beginning in the early decades of the nineteenth century with the preaching of the Wahhābi puritanism and revolt against saint-worship by such leaders as Sharī'at Allāh and Sayyid Ahmad of Rāi Barēli (killed in battle against the Sikhs in 1831), the movement gained a large following amongst Indian Muslims. Several organizations have explicitly carried on its principles, notably the fanatical Farā'idi sect in Bengal (who are also called Salafīya), and the more numerous congregations who call themselves Ahl-i-Hadīth, the Followers of the Prophetic Tradition, and maintain their own mosques and schools. But within the wider community as well, their campaign for the purification of doctrine and practice has found a ready response.

In this way the door was opened for the more personal and individual attempts to formulate Islamic doctrine in terms of modern thought. The first of these was made by Sir Sayyid Ahmad Khan (1817–98). Believing, like Shaikh Mohammed Abduh, that Islam and science could not prove antagonistic in the long run, he took the further step of asserting that the true justification of Islam was its conformity to Nature and the laws of science, and that nothing which conflicted with this principle could be regarded as authentically Islamic. In order to encourage and develop this line of thought, he founded at Aligarh in 1875 a college in which religious education should be combined with modern scientific studies, and thus established the first 'modernist' organization in Islam. The new college and its founder naturally became the target of violent opposition, and that not only from the orthodox Ulamā but also from Jamāl al-Dīn al-Afghāni, who bitterly attacked the *nēchari* philosophy as pure materialism and treason to the Faith. Nevertheless, the Aligarh movement prospered, though the college itself (which became in 1920 the Muslim University of Aligarh) has gradually moved away from its original doctrinal position.

The new liberalizing theology that followed from Sir Sayyid Ahmad Khan's rationalist approach to Islam, brought with it a re-valuation of the traditional social ethics of the Muslim community. The latter was probably one of its strongest attractions for the growing body of Muslim intellectuals, who were becoming acutely aware of the social evils linked with such practices as slavery and un-regulated polygamy and divorce. In this respect, indeed, the influence of his school extended far beyond the boundaries of Indian Islam through their new presentation, partly apologetic but also implicitly reformist, of Muslim practice and social doctrine.

Among the several Indian writers who popularized the new liberal theology and ethics, the leading figure was Sayyid Amīr Ali, a Shi'ite and a distinguished jurist. His book on *The Spirit of Islam,* first published in 1891, furnished the awakening political conscious-ness of Muslims with the reasoned basis of self-esteem which it required in face of the Western world. So exactly did it conform to the mood of his contemporaries that few educated Muslims observed that Amīr Ali was reformulating Islamic doctrine in terms of Western thought just as much as his *nēchari* predecessors had done. This is not the place to examine his positions in detail, but three of them must be mentioned because they have become integral elements of modern Muslim thought.

The first of these is the concentration, which we have already noted in other modern movements, upon the person of Mohammed. That the original title of *The Spirit of Islam* was *The Life and Teachings of Mohammed* is enough to show the central place of this theme in his exposition. But in contrast to the Sūfi doctrine of Mohammed it contains no hint of supernaturalism; Mohammed is presented as the embodiment and exemplar of human virtue in its most exalted manifestations. Amīr Ali himself carried his liberalism to the point of regarding the Koran as the work of Mohammed, but he has not been followed in this by the general body of modernists, who still maintain the orthodox doctrine of the Koran as the literal Word of God.

In the second place the teachings of Mohammed are presented in terms of contemporary social ideals. The four obligatory duties (prayer, fasting, almsgiving, and pilgrimage) are commended, rather than defended, on rational grounds of social and physical utility. The prevalence in Islamic society of slavery, polygamy, divorce by repudiation, and other moral and social weaknesses is admitted, but asserted to be contrary to the true teaching of the Koran, and responsibility for them is laid upon the later doctors and canonists. Slavery is held to be contrary to the Koranic teaching of the equality of all human beings; polygamy to be implicitly forbidden by the conditions attached to it in the Koran; divorce to be wholly opposed to the spirit of Mohammed's precept and example. In recent years many Muslim countries have passed civil legislation to tighten up the laws of marriage and divorce, as well as other branches of Shar'i law, administered in the Muslim religious courts, although only in Turkey have they been replaced by purely western codes. Slavery was abolished by law in all Muslim countries except Arabia in the second half of the nineteenth century.

The third point is the emphasis laid on Islam as a progressive civilizing force, the glories of Baghdad and Cordova, the advancement of learning and science, the religious tolerance and reception of Greek philosophy, the institution of hospitals and endowed schools. All this is contrasted with the contemporary life of medieval Europe, and it is believed with conviction by even highly educated Muslims that the revival of learning and the Renaissance in Europe were due to the stimulus of Islamic culture and the borrowing of its intellectual and technical skills by European scholars and craftsmen.

Apart from its apologetic and controversial uses, however, this argument serves to support two further modernist positions. One is that already taken up by Shaikh Mohammed Abduh, that Islam, rightly understood and practised, rejects any form of religious obscurantism and requires its adherents to pursue all branches of learning and science with their utmost endeavours. This is the riposte to the medieval depreciation of secular learning and the concentration of the Muslim madrasas upon theological and literary studies. Sanction is found for this doctrine in the frequent Koranic arguments from design and exhortations to study God's 'signs' in the natural world, and in several well-known sayings attributed to the Prophet, such as 'Seek knowledge, even unto China', and 'The ink of the scholar is more sacred than the blood of the martyr'.

The other position is that in taking over modern Western learning and science Muslims are only resuming the heritage of their own civilization. This argument has been most persuasively stated by Sir Mohammed Iqbāl (1876–1938), the exponent of the most sweeping modernist reformulation of Islamic doctrine. In contrast to the earlier modernists, the Muslim foundations of Iqbāl's theology are derived from Sūfistic philosophy, which he reinterpreted in terms of the Nietzschean superman and Bergson's theory of creative evolution. His own activist philosophy, which found expression first in a series of Persian and Urdu poems, made a powerful appeal to the younger generation of Indian Muslims and contributed to the rise of Pakistan as a Muslim state in 1947. It was given more systematic form in a series of lectures delivered in English in 1928 under the title of *The Reconstruction of Religious Thought in Islam,* but it is still doubtful how far it has gained a following outside Pakistan and India.

One further development within the Muslim community during the nineteenth century remains to be noted. This was the reappearance of the tendency to form new syncretist sects, a tendency manifested in the early centuries by the Nusairis, Druses, Yazīdis, and a number of Shi'ite sects, and at a later date by the Bektashis and the Sikh movement. There is no reason therefore to look for Western influences to explain their emergence. The first of the new sects, in fact, arose out of the Shaikhi philosophical school within Persian Shi'ism, and was led by Sayyid Ali Mohammed of Shīrāz. Calling himself by the old symbolic name of the *Bāb*, the 'gateway' through which divine truth is made known, he preached a combination of liberal religious doctrine with gnostic elements, and after a rising of his followers was executed in 1850.

The Babi sect broke in two after his death. The majority followed his disciple Bahā'ullāh (1817–92), who developed the original doctrine into a universal religion of pacifism and humanitarianism, called after himself Bahaism. The new religion, now definitely outside the pale of Islam, has had some success in Persia and the United States, and its headquarters are in Haifa in Palestine.

The only other syncretist movement of any importance arose in India out of a reaction to the 'Aligarh Movement'. Its leader, Mīrzā Ghulām Ahmad of Qādiān (d. 1908), claimed to be the bearer of a revelation to reinterpret Islam for the needs of a new age. Apart from this and his preaching of pacifism, his doctrines differed little from those of the moderate orthodox reformers who opposed saint-worship. He and the powerful organization which he built up were, however, vigorously attacked by the orthodox, mainly on the ground of his personal pretensions, and branded as heretics.

After the death of his first Khalīfa or successor in 1914, the Ahmadīya also split into two sections. The original or Qādiāni branch maintained the founder's claim to prophethood, and continued to recognize a Khalīfa; the seceders, or Lahore party, discarded both and formed themselves into a 'Society for the Propagation of Islam' under a new head. The Lahore branch subsequently endeavoured to become reconciled with orthodox Sunnism, though the Ulamā still regard them with some suspicion.

Both branches are distinguished for their extensive missionary activity, not only in India, but also in England and America. The Qadian party in particular are active opponents of Christian missions in the East Indies, and in South, East, and West Africa. The total number of their adherents cannot be estimated with any certainty, but even in India and Pakistan they are so few as to be relatively negligible against the mass of Indian Muslims.

Brief as this survey of the more recent developments within Islam has been, it has shown that the forces which shaped the religious attitude of Muslims in the past have lost none of their power. As in other historic religious communities, two opposed but complementary tendencies have been constantly in operation. One is the puritan reaction, the effort to hold fast to the legacy and tradition of the Medinian church and community, and unending struggle against 'innovations' which seem to menace the purity of primitive doctrine and practice. The other is the catholic tendency, which explicitly admits variety of opinion and usage in secondary matters, and implicitly accepts the necessity of reinterpretation to meet new and proved needs.

Many times already, Muslim religious leaders, confronted by the insistent demand of new modes of thought, have set themselves to the task of restating in their terms the eternal principles of the Koranic interpretation of the universe. We can, without exaggeration, speak of a Muslim Stoicism, a Muslim Aristotelianism, a Muslim Pantheism, all within the four corners of the orthodox community. The puritan reaction can never actually reverse this tendency and restore the primitive formulation and outlook; but it can and does destroy the compromises of the catholic spirit when these are felt to go so far as to become inconsistent with the basic religious experience of Islam. From its long inner history Islam has acquired both the adaptability and the toughness needed to meet the challenge of modern philosophical thought, although the terms of its reply have yet to be formulated.

Yet the dangers to which Islam, as a religion, is exposed today are perhaps greater than any that it has faced in the past. The most patent come from those forces which have undermined, or threaten to undermine, all theistic religion. The external pressure of secularism, whether in the seductive form of nationalism, or in the doctrines of scientific materialism and the economic interpretation of history, has already left its mark on several sections of Muslim society. But even this, however insidious its influence, is probably less dangerous in the long run than the relaxation of the religious conscience and the weakening of the catholic tradition of Islam.

Both these tendencies were accelerated by the breaking of the association between the religious orders and the Muslim middle and upper classes. Its place could not be taken by the Ulamā and the official organization, since the Ulamā have never sought or exercised that spiritual guidance and direction of the individual Believers which is part of the Christian pastorate. The new societies aimed, as we have seen, to supply some of the needs which had been met by the Sūfi orders, but with wide differences of emphasis. Recourse to organized effort was indeed needed to meet both the challenge of the outer world and the ravages of secularism within. The middle-class groups, however modernist and pacifist in tendency, have in general lacked the vitality to revive the lowered spiritual tension among the professional classes and have dwindled into coteries with little outward radiation. The 'Muslim Brotherhood' movement in Egypt, on the other hand, gained at first a wide popular following with its fundamentalist and activist programme, but fell victim eventually to the excesses of its extremist wing and was forcibly dissolved by government action in 1956. Such failures may not be decisive; nevertheless they tend to weaken still further the community of moral purpose and feeling within the Muslim world.

While this situation involves the Community as a whole, it lays a special responsibility upon the Ulamā. For their historic task has been to hold the balance between extremes, to preserve the stability and catholicity of the Community, and to regulate and represent its religious conscience. The impatience of would-be reformers with what they regard as the 'obscurantism' of the Ulamā is easy to understand. Tradition lies heavy upon them, as upon all convinced upholders of institutions whose roots, running deep into the centuries, are hidden beneath the surface of life. It would be difficult to deny in the majority of Ulamā a certain narrowness of outlook, an inability or even an unwillingness to realize the demands of the new life around them and to face the grave issues with which Muslim society is confronted.

Yet for all the faults that have been imputed to them with more or less justification, they have never yet as a body failed to serve the major religious interests of the Community. In spite of the tenacity inspired by their convictions and reinforced by their strong corporate sense, the absence of a hierarchy gives just enough resilience to prevent tenacity from passing into mere obstruction. If they are slow to follow changing fashions in thought and to pursue the immediate interests of dominant sections, by their long struggle against the secular governors and secular philosophies they have done much to protect the causes of religious and personal freedom. But faced with the changes of feeling around them in the world, they are being forced to return to the secular philosophies something of the earlier freedom which at one time was one of their factors of success. It is obvious that the 'science' of *hadīth* calls for determined action on the part of *Ulamā* and their ruthlessness in throwing out four-fifths of what passes for what Muhammad said. And it will take a century or more before the task is done. For it is the modern expansion of the State and of secular education in school and university that present the greatest challenges to the Ulamā of today. So long as they remain a class apart, with an educational system divorced from that of the main body of Muslims, their influence cannot but diminish. To the outside observer, it would seem that only if the Ulamā become again what they were in the historic Community, the nuclear body of 'learned men', leaders in its intellectual as well as spiritual life, can they effectively carry out their function and counteract the pressures that threaten to reduce Islam to a body of private beliefs without practical issue in social relations.

It is here that the point of crisis lies. Islam is a religion not only of the moral imperative but of that imperative embodied in the norms and way of life of a Community that embraces in principle all self-confessed Muslims. In former centuries the moral imperative, the Sacred Law, was spelled out in the classical Sharī'a. But to ardent reformers the slow processes of adjustment called for by the task of maintaining the cohesion of the Community are intolerable, and they look to the State to force the pace. Modern governments, therefore, when they legislate changes in the sphere of the Sharī'a have done so because by influential sections of contemporary Muslims the classical Sharī'a is regarded as no longer an adequate and sufficient interpretation of the moral imperative. Yet if the Sacred Law is wholly dethroned the link with the historic Community is broken; and the popular movements have demonstrated that the appeal to the Sharī'a can still be an effective instrument to energize the demand for social justice. Thus the task before the spiritual leadership of Islam today is not to fight a stubborn rearguard action, but to close the widening rifts within the Community by enlisting its creative participation in the effort to reformulate and reactivate the Sharī'a as a valid way of life in the new and changing conditions. The question is not one of refurbishing a time-encrusted methodology, nor on the other hand of transporting utilitarian or humanistic ethics into Islam from other systems. It is a question of the spiritual roots of life and action; and no Muslim people can shut itself off from the modern world, nor on the other hand sever its spiritual roots in the historic Community and remain a Muslim people in any effective sense. Unless the Ulamā are true to their office of maintaining an equal balance, and can satisfy the moral conscience of the most enlightened Muslims while yet, through all necessary changes, preserving the essence of the Islamic faith and ethic, they cannot safeguard the religious heritage of Islam from the corroding acids of our age.

Bibliography[1]

CHAPTER I

R. A. NICHOLSON: *A Literary History of the Arabs* (2nd ed., Cambridge 1930)
  The best introduction to Islamic culture for English readers. On the Persian side it should be supplemented by—

E. G. BROWNE: *A Literary History of Persia* (4 vols., London and Cambridge 1902–24)

SIR WILLIAM MUIR: *The Caliphate : Rise, Decline and Fall* (revised ed., Edinburgh 1915 etc.)

P. K. HITTI: *History of the Arabs* (London and New York 1937; 5th ed. 1951)
  The standard English histories of medieval Islamic civilization.

B. LEWIS: *The Arabs in History* (London 1950)
  A balanced and readable general survey, brought down to modern times.

SIR T. W. ARNOLD: *The Caliphate* (Oxford 1924)

R. LEVY: *The Social Structure of Islam* (Cambridge 1958)

S. LANE-POOLE: *A History of Egypt in the Middle Ages* (2nd ed., London 1914 etc.)
  History and civilization of Muslim Egypt to 1517.

P. WITTEK: *The Rise of the Ottoman Empire* (London 1938)
  Short but valuable study of the interaction of religion and politics.

SIR T. W. ARNOLD: *The Preaching of Islam* (2nd ed., London 1913)
  The best general account of the religious expansion of Islam.

The Encyclopaedia of Islam (4 vols. and Supplement, Leyden 1913–38. New edition now proceeding)
  An indispensable (though unequal) work of reference on Islamic religion, history, literature etc.

---

[1] Except for a few standard authorities in other European languages, the bibliography is confined to works published in English.

The Shorter Encyclopaedia of Islam (Leyden 1953)
  Reprint, with revisions, of the articles on religion and law in the *Encyclopaedia of Islam*.

T. P. HUGHES: *A Dictionary of Islam* (London 1885 and 1935)
  Still a useful reference work for Muslim religion and law, especially in India.

The Legacy of Islam, ed. Sir T. W. Arnold and A. Guillaume (Oxford 1931)
  Articles on Islamic religious thought, science, and art, and their influence upon Europe.

L. MASSIGNON: *Annuaire du Monde Musulman* (Paris 1955 (latest issue))
  Data relative to the history, population, organization, etc. of all countries with Muslim populations.

CHAPTERS 2, 3, 4

W. MONTGOMERY WATT: *Muhammad at Mecca* (Oxford 1953)

—— *Muhammad at Medina* (Oxford 1958)
  Most up-to-date discussion of the Prophet.

TOR ANDRAE: *Mohammed, The Man and his Faith*, English trans. (London 1936)
  Good short presentation of recent research.

—— *Die Person Mohammeds in Lehre und Glauben seiner Gemeinde* (Stockholm 1918)
  A study of the development of Muslim conceptions of and attitude towards the Prophet.

J. C. ARCHER: *Mystical Elements in Mohammed* (Yale University Press 1924)
  Brings out much-neglected aspect of Mohammed's character and teaching.

The Koran
  The older English translations by GEORGE SALE (Chandos Classics), J. M. RODWELL (Everyman's Library), and E. H. PALMER (Worlds Classics) are all rather literal and inadequate. A more recent version is:

A. J. ARBERRY: *The Koran Reinterpreted* (London 1955)
  In fact, however, no translation is fully satisfactory.

R. BELL: *The Qur'ān* (2 vols., Edinburgh 1937–9)
  The first attempt at a critical arrangement of the contents of each sūra.

A. YUSUF ALI: *The Holy Quran* (2 vols., Lahore 1934)
  An Indian 'modernist' interpretation.

TH. NÖLDEKE: *Geschichte des Qorans* (2nd ed., 3 vols., Leipzig 1909–38)

R. BLACHÈRE: *Introduction au Coran* (Paris 1947)
  Standard work on the history of the Koran.

R. BELL: *The Origin of Islam in its Christian Environment* (London 1926)
  A study of the influence of Syrian Christianity on Mohammed's religious ideas.

SYED AMEER ALI: *The Spirit of Islam* (Revised ed., London 1922)
   A modernist presentation of Mohammed's life and teachings (see pp. 182–3).

H. U. W. STANTON: *The Teaching of the Qur'ān* (S.P.C.K. 1919)
   A useful summary of Koranic doctrine.

R. ROBERTS: *The Social Laws of the Qorân* (London 1925)
   The relevant Koranic passages, with their legal development, and comparison with the legislation of the Old Testament.

CHAPTERS 5, 6, 7

D. B. MACDONALD: *Development of Muslim Theology, Jurisprudence, and Constitutional Theory* (London and New York 1903 etc.)

H. LAMMENS: *Islam, Beliefs and Institutions*, trans. by Sir E. D. Ross (London 1929)
   Good general sketches of the whole field.

I. GOLDZIHER: *Muhammedanische Studien*, vol. II (Halle 1890)
   The standard critical study of the Hadīth. (The early publication of English and French translations of this work is expected.)

A. GUILLAUME: *The Traditions of Islam* (Oxford 1924)
   An introduction, based in part on the preceding.

M. MUHAMMAD ALI: *A Manual of Hadīth* (Lahore n.d.)
   Annotated selection from al-Bukhāri and later works.

A. J. WENSINCK: *The Muslim Creed* (Cambridge 1932)
   Critical analysis of early statements of orthodox doctrine to show its growth and development in reaction to heretical and Mu'tazilite positions.

D. S. MARGOLIOUTH: *The Early Development of Mohammedanism* (London 1914)
   A valuable, though sceptical, study of the expansion of theology, law and ethics.

W. MONTGOMERY WATT: *Free Will and Predestination in Early Islam* (London 1948)
   A more perceptive analysis of this problem.

L. GARDET et M. M. ANAWATI: *Introduction à la Théologie musulmane* (Paris 1948)
   Discussion of the developed theological system from a Thomist angle.

D. M. DONALDSON: *The Shi'ite Religion* (London 1933)
   The general development of Shi'ite theology, preceded by uncritical accounts of the Shi'ite Imāms.

A. A. A. FYZEE: *A Shi'ite Creed* (O.U.P., London 1942)
   Annotated translation of the treatise of Ibn Bābawaih (d. 991).

B. Lewis: *The Assassins* (London 1967)
A clear and level-headed guide through a complicated subject.

M. G. S. Hodgson: *The Order of Assassins* (The Hague 1955)

R. J. McCarthy: *The Theology of al-Ash'ari* (Beirut 1953)

F. Rahman: *Prophecy in Islam* (London 1958)

T. J. de Boer: *The History of Philosophy in Islam,* trans. by E. R. Jones (London 1903 etc.)
Outlines of the main philosophical systems in the medieval Islamic civilization.

A. A. A. Fyzee: *Outlines of Muhammadan Law* (O.U.P., London 1949).
A general introduction to the subject.

Syed Ameer Ali: *Personal Law of the Mahommedans* (London 1880)
A more detailed treatment of the actual application of the law of personal status.

L. Ostrorog: *The Angora Reform* (London 1927)
Three lectures, including an excellent discussion on the 'roots of law' which has been largely drawn upon in Chapter 6.

D. Santillana: *Instituzioni di diritto musulmano malichita* (2 vols., Rome 1926–38)
The best general survey of the structure and contents of Islamic Law (Māliki and Shāfi'i schools).

J. Schacht: *The Origins of Muhammadan Jurisprudence* (Oxford 1950)
A pioneer work on the early schools of law and the development of legal theory.

CHAPTERS 8 AND 9

R. A. Nicholson: *The Mystics of Islam* (London 1914)
The best short introduction to the subject.

— — *The Idea of Personality in Sūfism* (Cambridge 1923)
A caution against over-emphasis on the pantheistic element in Sūfi thought.

— — *Studies in Islamic Mysticism* (Cambridge 1921)
Studies of the works of three representative Sūfis. In addition, Professor Nicholson has translated the *Kashf al-Mahjūb* of al-Hujwīri (d. 1072) (London 1911 and 1936), the mystical odes of Ibn al-Arabi (London 1911), a selection from the odes of Jalāl al-Dīn al-Rūmi (*Dīvāni Shamsi Tabrīz,* Cambridge U.P. 1898), and the same poet's *Mathnawi* with a Commentary (8 vols., London 1925–40). Other works on individual mystics are:

A. J. Arberry: *The Mawāqif of al-Niffarī* (London 1935)

MARGARET SMITH: *Rabi'a the Mystic* (Cambridge 1928)

—— *An early Mystic of Baghdad* (London 1935)
A study of the writings of al-Muhāsibi (d. 857).

A. J. WENSINCK: *La Pensée de Ghazzali* (Paris 1940)
Several sections of Ghazāli's *Ihyā 'Ulūm ad-Dīn* have been translated.

L. MASSIGNON: *Al-Hallaj, Martyr mystique de l'Islam* (2 vols., Paris 1922)
A penetrating study of the founder of Sūfi theology.

—— *Essai sur les Origines de Lexique technique de la Mystique musulmane* (Paris 1922)
The basic work on the origins of Sūfism.

A. J. ARBERRY: *Sūfism* (London 1950)
Brief but masterly historical survey, with translated extracts from Sūfi writings and poems.

A. E AFFIFI: *The Mystical Philosophy of Muhyid Din-ibnul Arabi* (Cambridge 1939)
An attempt to reduce Ibn al-Arabi's writings to an orderly system.

O. DEPONT et X. COPPOLANI: *Les Confréries religieuses musulmanes* (Algiers 1897)
The only work which attempts to cover the history of the Sūfi orders, with special reference to North Africa.

J. K. BIRGE: *The Bektashi Order of Dervishes* (London 1937)
A detailed account of the history, doctrines, and practices of this syncretist order.

CHAPTER 10

H. ST. J. B. PHILBY: *Arabia* (London 1930)
The fullest account in English of the Wahhābi movement.

E. G. BROWNE: *The Persian Revolution of 1905–1909* (Cambridge 1910)
Chapter I contains a biography of Jamāl al-Dīn al-Afghāni.

C. C. ADAMS: *Islam and Modernism in Egypt* (O.U.P., London 1933)
A detailed study of the movement associated with Jamāl al-Dīn, Mohammed Abduh, and the Salafīya group.

H. A. R. GIBB (ed.): *Whither Islam?* (London 1932)
Four lectures on Muslim movements in North Africa, Egypt, India, and Indonesia, with introduction and conclusion.

MURRAY TITUS: *Indian Islam* (O.U.P., London 1930)
A useful compilation of data relating to Islam in India.

W. C. SMITH: *Modern Islam in India* (2nd ed., London 1946)
A socio-religious analysis of recent intellectual and political movements amongst Muslims.

—— *Islam in Modern History* (Princeton 1957)

SIR MOHAMMAD IQBAL: *The Secrets of the Self*, trans. by R. A. Nicholson (London 1920)
Iqbal's first poetical exposition of his philosophy, with an introduction by the translator.

—— *The Reconstruction of Religious Thought in Islam* (2nd ed., O.U.P., London 1934)
See pages 126–7.

H. A. R. GIBB: *Modern Trends in Islam* (Chicago 1947)
A critique of Islamic modernism.

W. M. MILLER: *Bahaism, its Origin, History, Teachings* (New York 1931)

C. SNOUCK HURGRONJE: *The Achehnese* (2 vols., Leyden 1906)
The outstanding work on modern Muslim sociology and religion in Indonesia.

A. H. HOURANI: *Syria and Lebanon* (O.U.P., London 1946)
Includes a valuable analysis of the effects of Western penetration on Muslim thought and institutions.

J. M. B. BALYON: *Modern Muslim Koran Interpretation 1880–1960* (Leyden 1961)

F. RAHMAN: *Islam* (London 1966)

G. E. VON GRUNEBAUM: *Modern Islam* (California 1962)

AZIZ AHMAD: *Islamic Modernism in India and Pakistan 1857–1964* (Oxford 1967)
All four give various interpretations of religious and legal thought in recent essays.

Index

Abbasid Caliphs, 5, 7, 58, 59, 69, 75
Abd al-Aziz Āl Su'ūd, 114
Abd al-Ghani al-Nābulusi, 111
ablutions, 43, 61
Abraham, 26, 32, 40
Abu Bakr, 21, 22, 82
Abu Dāwud, 55
Abu Hanīfa, 69, 77
Abu Madyan, 107, 108
Abu Yūsuf, 69
Abyssinia, 19, 26
'acquisition', 79
Adam, 39, 62, 84
adhān, 43
Afghans, Afghanistan, 13, 15
Africa, 8, 10, 13, 14, 15, 70, 97, 115, 116, 117, 128; *see also* North Africa
Ahl-i Hadīth, 123
Ahmad ibn Hanbal, 59, 70, 80
Ahmad ibn Idrīs, 116–17
Ahmad al-Bedawi, 106
Ahmad al-Rifā'i, 106
Ahmad Sarhindi, 111
Ahmadīya, 127
Ahmadīya order, 106
A'isha, 55
'ālam al-mithāl, 111
Alexander legend, 28
Alī, 50, 59, 82, 83, 84, 85, 105
Alī Mohammed, Sayyid, 127
Aligarh, 124, 127
Allāh, 26, 31, 36–8; attributes of, 76, 79, 85; speech of, 76

Almohads, 107
Almoravids, 107
alms, 27, 29, 43–4
alūfa, 107
America, 15, 127, 128
Amīr Ali, Sayyid, 124–5
al-Amīr Ghani, 117
Amīrghanīya order, 118
Angels, 38–9
Arab Empire, 2–4, 74
Arabian culture, 5–7, 23, 25–7, 31, 32, 47, 50, 69–70
Arafāt, 44
asceticism, 27, 33, 87–8, 90, 93, 100
al-Ash'ari, Ash'arite theology, 79, 80, 95–6
Asīr, 117
'Assassins', 85
Avempace, Averroes, Avicenna, 81
al-Awzā'i, 70
al-Azhar mosque, 98, 120

bāb, 53, 127
babas, 109
Babism, 112, 127
Badr, 20, 39
Bahā'ullah, Bahaism, 127
al-Baidāwi, 35
al-Bakri, Mustafa, 111
baraka, 107
Bayyūmi order, 106
Bedawīya order, 106–7

Bedouin (tribesmen), 3, 8–9, 20, 32, 47, 60, 73, 75
Bektashis, 108–9, 127
Berbers, 8, 14, 15, 107, 115–16
bē-sharʿ, 109
biḍʿa (innovation), 50, 67, 96, 114, 128
Bilāl, 43
Black Stone, 44
al-Bukhāri, 52, 53, 54, 55, 57

'Calenders', 109
Caliphate, Caliphs, 3, 10–11, 66, 67, 71, 74, 75, 82, 83, 85, 120, 121; see also Abbasid, Fatimid, Umayyad
Carmathians, 85
celibacy, 93
China, 10, 14, 15, 126
Chishti order, 109
circumcision, 43n.
Companions of the Prophet, 23, 33, 51–3, 58, 74, 82, 117
Creed, Mohammedan, 2, 36

daʿīf, 53
darwīsh, 103, 104, 105, 109, 110
Dasūqi order, 106
Da'ud al-Zāhiri, 70
David, 28, 40
Derqāwa, 108
devils, 39
dhikr, 90, 92, 96, 104, 106, 108, 117
Dhu'l-Qarnain, 40
'Ditch', Battle of the, 20
divorce, 22, 46, 124, 125
dowries, 46
Druses, 127
dualism, 74, 75, 77

East Indies, see Indonesia
ecstasy, 94, 101
education, 98, 111, 118, 120, 124, 125, 126, 130
Era, Mohammedan, 2
ethics, 29, 46, 49, 69, 78, 79, 111, 124

faqīr, 103, 109
al-Fārābi, 81
Farā'idi sect, 123
fasting, 30, 44

fātihah, 42
Fātima, 84
Fātimid Caliphate, 85, 98
fatwā, 71
fiqh, 61
freewill, 27, 76, 77, 79

Gabriel, 24, 39, 55
gambling, 46
al-Ghazāli, 94–5, 97, 100, 101, 102, 115, 121
Ghulām Ahmad, Mirza, 127
ghusl, 43
Gnosticism, 73, 75, 85, 88, 89, 94, 100, 105, 108
Goddesses, Meccan, 31, 37
Gog and Magog, 40
Greek science, 5–6; see also Philosophy

hadd, 68
Hadīth, 4, 21–2, 24, 49 sqq., 61–7, 70, 74, 79, 80, 123
Hāfiz, 101
al-Hallāj, 89, 90, 91
Hanafi school, 69, 70
Hanbali school, 70, 114, 117; 'Neo-Hanbalites', 122
Hanīfiyya, 26
hanīfs, 26, 31
al-Haqq, 102
hasan, 53
al-Hasan of Basra, 56, 77, 88
Hell, 41–2, 48, 57, 95
Hellenistic culture, 3, 4, 5, 6, 75–6, 77–9, 83, 87; see also philosophy
heresy, heretics, 4, 9, 67, 75, 76, 87, 91, 92, 97, 98
Hijra, 2, 18
hikma, 63
Hinduism, 109
hospitals, 126
Hūd, 26

'ibādāt, 42, 61
Iblīs, 39
Ibn 'Abbās, 55–6
Ibn al-Arabi, 101, 107, 111
Ibn Māja, 55
Ibn Sa'd, 52

Ibn Taimīya, 110, 114
Ibn Tūmart, 107
Idrīsīya order, 117
ihrām, 44
ijāza, 98
ijmā', 65, 66, 67, 70, 96, 116–17
ijtihād, 66, 71, 122
'ilm, 61, 93
images, 1–2, 46
imām, 43
Imāmīs, 84, 85, (111)
Imāms, 83–4, 85
India, Indians, 3, 8, 10, 12, 13, 15, 82, 85, 97, 109–10, 111, 114, 116, 123, 127–8
Indian culture, 5, 82
Indian Mutiny, 120
Indonesia, 10, 14, 15, 70, 97, 106, 123, 128
Inheritance, 46
'innovation', *see bid'a*
Intercession, 42, 79, 116
Iqbāl, Muhammad, 110, 126
Īsāwīya order, 108
Ishmael, 31–2
Islām, 2
Ismā'īlis, 84–5, 100
isnād, 52, 55, 56, 57, 58

Ja'far al-Sādiq, 85
Ja'fari school, 85
Jalāl ad-Dīn al-Rūmi, 102, 109, 115
Jamāl al-Dīn Afghāni, 120, 122, 124
Jāmi, 102
Jesus, 28, 31, 37, 39, 40, 41, 88, 89
jihād, 45, 117
al-Jīlāni, Abd, al-Qādir, 105, 106
jinn, 39, 41
John the Baptist, 28, 40
Joseph, 28, 40

Kaaba, 44
kāhins, 25
Khadīja, 17
Khalīfa, 103; *see also* Caliphate
Khalwatīya order, 111, 116
khāngāh, 103
Khārijite sect, 75, 77, 81, 107
al-Khidr, 40

al-Kindi, 81
kitāb, 50, 63
Koran: compilation, 24–5, 33, 48; interpretation, 34–5, 65, 67, 83, 88, 101, 115, 120, 122, 128; reciters and recitation, 34; 'uncreated', 76; variant readings, 34

Last Judgement, 26, 28, 37, 41–2, 88, 90
Law, Islamic, 3, 5, 7, 9, 11, 12, 22, 46, 52, 53, 55, 58, 60–72, 82, 85, 92, 119, 121, 122, 131; Schools of, 35, 53, 60, 69–71
Law, Roman, 7, 60–1, 69–70
Law, Western, 121
Libya, 117, 118
Light philosophy, 84, 85, 89
'Light-verse', 38
Lot, 28
Luqmān, 40

madhhab, 70, 71
madrasas, 98, 100
Mahdi, 58, 88, 118
'Mahomet', 1
Majlisi, Moh. Bāqir, 111
Malaya, Malays, 14–15
Mālik ibn Anas, 70
Māliki school, 70
Mamlūks, 11–12
al-Manār, 122
Mandingos, 14
marabouts, 107
ma'rifa, 93
martyrs, 42, 46
Marwān, 84
Mary, (30), 37, 40
mathematics, 5, 6
al-Māturīdi, 79
mazālim, 71
medical science, 5, 6
Melāmīya, 110
Mevlevīya, 109
Michael, 39
minarets, 43
modernism, 120–2, 123, 124–7, 129
Mohammed ibn Abd al-Wahhāb, 114
Mohammed Abduh, 120–1, 122, 124, 126

Mohammed al-Muntazar, 84
Mongols, 11, 12, 14, 106 108
Morocco, 3, 14, 82, 107, 108, 122
Moses, 31, 40
mosque, 43
mu'ezzin, 43
mufti, 71
Mughal Empire, 12, 13, 109
Muhammadīya order, 117
Mu'īn al-Din Chishti, 109
mujtahid, 66, 85
Mullā Sadrā, 111
murīd, 102
Murji'ites, 77
al-Murtadā, Mohammed, 115
musalmān, musulman, 1
muslim, 1, 2
Muslim (traditionist), 53, 55
Muslim Brotherhood, 123
Muslims, numbers of, 15
Mu'tazilite school, 75–80, 87, 95

Names of God, 36
Naqshbandī order, 109, 111
al-Nasā'i, 55
nēchari philosophy, 124–5
Negroes, 14, 15, 107, 116; *see also* Africa
Neoplatonism, 100, 101
Nizām ul Mulk, 80
Noah, 28, 40
nomads, 7–9, 10, 81; *see also* Bedouins
North Africa, North-west Africa, 5, 8, 12, 13, 15, 70, 82, 97, 107–8, 116
Nubia, 118
Nusairis, 127

Ohod, 20
Oman, 82
Omar, 54, 82
Othmān, 33, 82
Ottoman Empire, 12, 13, 14, 71, 108, 109, 110, 114, 118, 120

Pakistan, 15, 70, 123, 126–7
Pan-Islamism, 120, 122
pantheism, 99, 101
Paradise, 41, 48
'Perfect Man', 101

persecution, 75, 79
Persia, Persians, 2, 3, 5, 8, 12, 13, 15, 19, 21, 73, 80, 82, 83, 84, 97, 98, 101, 101–2, 111, 115, 120, 126, 127
Persian culture, 3, 5, 12, 82, 102
Philippine Is., 15
Philosophy, Greek, 1, 6, 51, 60, 75–6, 78–81, 96, 126
Philosophy, Islamic, 77–8, 80–1, 111, 126, 128
Philosophy, Western, 119, 126, 128–9
pilgrimage, 32, 44–5, 47
'Pilgrimage, Farewell', 29
Pillars of Faith, 45, 68, 85
pīr, 102, 103
polygamy, 22, 124, 125
prayer, 27, 29, 30, 33, 42–3, 61
predestination, 27, 38, 76–80
Prophets, 2, 26, 28, 31, 39–41, 62, 63, 84, 127
Psalms, 40
Pure Brethren, Epistles of the, 100

qādī, 71
Qādirīya order, 105, 108, 109, 116
Qalandari order, 109
qānūn, 61
Qarmatis, 85, 103
qibla, 43
qiyās, 64, 70, 117
al-Qushairi, 94
quṣṣās, 88, 92
quṭb, 94

Rābi'a al-Adawīya, 90
ar-Rahmān, 28
rak'ah, 42
Ramadān, 44
Rashīd, House of, 114
Rashīd Ridā, 122
rationalism, 6, 76–80, 124
ra'y, 70
al-Rāzi, 35
reformist movements, 116, 117, 120–7, 129
Renaissance, 99, 126
Resurrection, 18, 27, 41
retaliation, 22
ribāt, 103

Rifā'īya order, 106

Sacred Months, 45
sadaqāt, 43, 44
Safavid dynasty, 12, 111
sahīh, 53, 57
al-Sahīh, 53-5, 56, 57
Saints, saint-worship, 23, 93, 103, 107,
    108, 109, 114, 116, 122, 123, 127
Sajjādeh-nishīn, 103
Salafīya, 122-3
Salmān, 105
sama', 90, 92
Saudi Arabia, 114
Sayyid Ahmad, 123
Sayyid Ahmad Khān, 124
Sayyid Amīr Ali, 124-5
Scriptures, 40-1
sects, 35, 51, 58, 81-5, 111
Senussis, see Sunūsīya order
Seven Sleepers, 28, 40
al-Shādhili, 108
Shādhilīya order, 108, 117
al-Shāfi'i, 70
Shāfi'i school, 70, 80
Shāh Walī-Allāh, 111
shahāda, 36, 42, 45
al-Shaibāni, 69
Shaikh Ahmad, Shaikhīya sect, 111,
    127
Shaikh al-Islām, 71
Shaikh Saddū, 109
shaikhs, sūfi, 93, 97, 103-4
shaitāns, 39
Shamanism, 106, 108
sharī'a, 64; see Law, Islamic
sharī'at Allāh, 123
Shī'a, Shi'ism, 13, 50, 58-9, 80, 82-5,
    88, 91, 97, 100, 103, 105, 107, 108,
    111, 124, 127
shirk, 37
Shu'aib, 26
Sikhs, 123, 127
sinlessness, 84-5
slavery, slave trade, 14, 124, 125
societies, religious, 123, 129
Solomon, 28, 39
Spanish-Arabic culture, 5, 7, 13, 101,
    126

Sudan, 15, 118
Sūfi, Sūfism, 9, 11, 12, 23, 59, 85, 89-
    111, 114, 115, 116, 117, 122, 125, 126;
    see also Saints
Sultans, Sultanate, 8, 9, 11, 14, 71
Sulu archipelago, 14
sunna, Sunni, 50-1
al-Sunūsi, Mohammed, 117
Sunūsīya order, 118
sūras of the Koran, 24, 28-33
Su'ūd, House of, 114
swine's flesh, 46
syncretism, 127

al-Tabari, 35, 58
al-Tabarsi, 35
taqīya, 85
tarīqa, 103; see also Sūfism
tekke, 109
'Throne-verse', 37
al-Tījāni, Tījānīya order, 116
Timur (Tamerlane), 12, 97
al-Tirmidhi, 55
Tradition, see Hadīth
Turkey, Turkish Republic, 13, 15, 109,
    121, 122, 125, 130
Turks, 8, 11, 13, 15, 97, 101, 108-9,
    115; see also Ottoman Empire
'Two-horned, The', 28, 40

Ulamā, 65
Umayyad Caliphs, 4, 5, 33, 43, 59, 60,
    69, 78, 82, 84
U.S.S.R., 15
usury, 46

Wahhābis, 71, 82, 114, 115, 116, 122,
    123
Western Civilization, 113, 118-20, 121,
    122, 123, 125, 126
wine, 46
women, status of, 22, 93, 108, 124, 125
wudhū, 43

Yazīd, 84
Yazīdīs, 84, 127
Yemen, 26, 84, 115
Yesevīya order, 108
Yūsuf al-Kūmi, 108

Zāhiri school, 70, 108
Zaidis, 84
zakāh, 43–4
al-Zamakhshari, 35

Zanzibar, 15, 82
Zechariah, 40
Zoroastrianism, 3, 83, 88